W9-ARE-754

PHOTOGRAPHY
On The Go
ROBT. L. WHITBY   WA 6-3049

Spanish: Contemporary Methodology

A BLAISDELL BOOK
IN THE MODERN LANGUAGES

CONSULTING EDITOR

Charles N. Staubach

University of Arizona

David M. Feldman
Walter D. Kline

CALIFORNIA STATE COLLEGE AT FULLERTON

Spanish:
CONTEMPORARY
METHODOLOGY

DOWNS JONES LIBRARY
HUSTON-TIL...

Blaisdell Publishing Company
A DIVISION OF GINN AND COMPANY

WALTHAM, MASSACHUSETTS | TORONTO | LONDON

PC 4065
F43

Copyright © 1969 by Blaisdell Publishing Company,
A Division of Ginn and Company.
All rights reserved. No part of the material covered by
this copyright may be produced in any form or by any
means of reproduction.
Library of Congress Catalog Card Number: 69-17275
Printed in the United States of America.

Preface

Ever since the principles of the Army Specialized Training Program were introduced into American educational life in the instruction of modern foreign languages during the Second World War, there has been a constant effort to improve and refine methods of teaching foreign languages. The past two decades have seen the extensive publication of works dealing with the various aspects of language learning and teaching, and textbooks reflecting significant advances in the presentation of the spoken language in the most productive and efficient format. The advent of these teaching texts and methodological works has been made possible largely through remarkable advances in the science of linguistics and has led not only to a whole new body of specially designed supplementary electromechanical aids, but also to a renewed awareness of the cultural aspects of foreign language study. It has become truly impossible to discuss any one of the aspects of today's approaches to language teaching without considering all its other concomitants.

The present-day teacher of modern foreign languages may read with profit and interest in the opening chapter of this book about the wide variety of methods which have been practiced throughout the history of foreign language teaching in the United States. Each of these methods or approaches contributed meaningfully to the development of successful language teaching and helped to pave the way for those new insights into the nature of language learning processes which have resulted in the prevalence of the "fundamental skills" method. The latter con-

75994

stitutes the main concern of this book: the teaching of Spanish in an approach which emphasizes the fundamental skills of listening comprehension, speaking, reading, and writing, presented in an ordered sequence and set forth in an inductive learning experience.

These principles underlie an approach to foreign language teaching that has been given many different names, one of the most common of which is "audio-lingual." But as is pointed out in Chapter 1, the inadequacy suggested by that term and the confusion occasioned by it have led recent writers on the subject to suggest a new name: fundamental skills method. The name is unimportant, however, as long as the principles mentioned above constitute the foundation of the approach, and although new theories and new approaches to language structure, such as the generative transformational model, have promised to add new dimensions to what is now being done, it still appears that the present methodology will continue to be based on the idea of the four skills, presented in order and in an inductive format.

Today's foreign language teacher, then, no matter what he calls the method he uses, cannot fail to profit from the basic principles discussed in this book, because any approach may be strengthened by their application. Prospective teachers will also gain considerably from a close examination of the theory and techniques which have been evolved recently.

The effective foreign language teacher is one who is competently proficient in the target language and fully cognizant of the most effective means of developing all language skills in his students by the ordered contextual presentation and drill of language structures. Consequently, we have devoted several chapters of this book to the basic problems of pronunciation, syntactical drills, testing, and the language laboratory. But the use of these techniques is not complete unless the teacher has some comprehension of the linguistic bases for them and an adequate understanding of the relative importance of the reading and writing skills and the acquisition of cultural insights in the total language program as it is envisioned in the secondary school sequence of today. These aspects are the subjects of yet further chapters.

We have consistently attempted to emphasize the practical. At the conclusion of each chapter are exercises which provide the opportunity to explore the concepts in greater detail. The literature in the field already contains an abundance of excellent works on applied linguistics, the theory of second language learning, the physical requirements of the language laboratory, etc., and it is not our intention to duplicate them. Many of the best of these works are listed in the bibliography at the end of each chapter, leading the reader to some of the more relevant literature which may be useful in putting into practice the theories synthesized here.

Neither do we conceive of this book as a "do-it-yourself kit." It is, rather, a practical survey of the components of contemporary methodology. It may stand by itself, help the teacher to enrich his present knowledge, or combine into a unified whole the many ideas which he may already have concerning the various aspects of language teaching. For example, we do not exhaust the subject of pattern drills and the linguistic analysis of structure which underlies them, but, once the reader has applied his own experience and knowledge to what is contained here, he will have a sound basis for a richer comprehension of his later readings.

The authors believe that the reader will also find here a practical synthesis of the material found in several excellent books in the field of contemporary methodology. Many of the ideas and techniques have, of course, been considered in those other works and have played a vital role in the classroom procedures of many of the most effective teachers in recent years. Others, however, are new, and an overall understanding of their application may lead to even greater improvement in language teaching.

The authors wish to express their thanks to their friend and colleague Gustave Mathieu for permission to reprint his materials. To Charles Staubach the authors owe a special debt of gratitude for his many invaluable suggestions in the preparation of the final manuscript and for his constant encouragement.

D.M.F.
W.D.K.

Contents

Spanish: Contemporary Methodology

1

$\mathcal{P}$erspectives in foreign language teaching

Today's approach to language teaching, no matter how revolutionary it may appear, has its origins in the nineteenth century. It was in that period, characterized by the elaboration of the evolutionary postulate, that the whole study of man, his culture, and his behavior became the object of intense study. Naturally, the study of language (man's first and most important invention) became central. What linguists and anthropologists set out to do at that time became the foundation of all modern linguistic investigation: to discover the nature of communication in culture groups and to examine minutely, without puristic bias, the structure of language as it was spoken, as it was used to communicate. This, however, could not be accomplished until the literary and historical aspects of language, which had previously been the main concern of philological investigation, were transcended. This rapidly expanding study of human communication led linguists to direct their attention to the problem of teaching a given system of communication to people who used a different system; that is, to teach one language to speakers of another.

Basic to this new pedagogy was an idea which has, through steady repetition, become almost a platitude: human communicative behavior is first of all spoken, and only secondarily written. Nevertheless, no matter how often we reiterate this concept, we still find it difficult to apply in practice. It is all too easy to recognize the essentially oral nature of language from an abstract point of view and then to relapse into written language approaches in our actual instructional procedures. Consequently, we must constantly remind ourselves that spoken language is as old as man himself, while writing, to the contrary, has a history of a few thousand years, at most. Speech is prior to writing in every sense, but literate societies still consistently confuse the two. Although in our society reading and writing are the basic attributes of the "educated" man, our primary concern throughout this book is the teaching of the spoken language.

The history of foreign language teaching in the United States has been summarized elsewhere.[1] Major ethnic groups in the colonial and immediate post-colonial periods provided sporadic instruction for their own children in the language of their own national origins, such as the French Catholic missionaries in what is now northern New England, the Spanish-speaking Catholic missionaries in what is now the American southwest, and the German-speaking settlers in Pennsylvania. French and German did not join the trio of "classical" languages — Latin, Greek, and Hebrew — in the academies and universities until the eighteenth century. Even though French and German were modern spoken languages, in teaching them the emphasis was as unremittingly literary as it was in the case of the "classical" languages, focusing solely on the development of reading, writing, and translating abilities in the students.

The "natural" and "direct" methods, imported from Europe, succeeded in introducing some oral techniques in foreign language teaching as early as 1866, but neither approach was able to counterbalance the established weight of the "grammar-translation" tradition in American schools.

Thus, the first century and a quarter of American national educational life saw little fundamental change either in the selection of languages taught in schools and colleges or in the approach to teaching them.

[1] Edmond A. Méras, *A Language Teacher's Guide*, 2nd ed. (New York: Harper and Row, 1962), pp. 1–8; 32–52. Peter Hagboldt, "The Teaching of Languages from the Middle Ages to the Present" in *The Teaching of German* (Boston: D. C. Heath, 1940). William G. Moulton, *Linguistics and Language Teaching in the United States 1940–1960* (Washington, D.C.: Government Printing Office, 1963). Edwin H. Zeydel, *The Teaching of German in the United States* (New York: Modern Language Association, 1962). Jefferson R. Spell, "Spanish Teaching in the United States" (*Hispania X*, 1927, pp. 141–159). George B. Watts, "The Teaching of French in the United States" (*French Review XXXVII*, 1963, pp. 1–165). W. H. Bruford, *First Steps in German Fifty Years Ago* (New York: MLA, 1965). Sturgis Leavitt, *The Teaching of Spanish in the United States* (New York: MLA, 1961).

Despite the massive exposure of Americans to Europe during World War I, language teaching in the period between the two wars continued to limit its objectives to providing a reading knowledge of a foreign language. A two-year exposure was generally considered sufficient. Little progress had been made in expanding the number of languages taught: Latin, French, and Spanish predominated in the schools; the same, plus Greek and German, in the colleges. Opportunities for studying other languages did exist, of course, but they were severely limited in number, and few students were able to take advantage of them.

The outbreak of World War II and the attack on Pearl Harbor in 1941 occasioned the creation of new methods of foreign language teaching. It was realized that within a short time large numbers of American soldiers would be sent to various parts of the world where they would need fluency in one or more foreign languages, often under difficult conditions. Because the schools and colleges had failed to produce persons capable of communicating orally in even the most familiar languages, the armed services determined to begin an intensive and extensive program of language training different from any as yet known in the United States.

A model for this undertaking was provided by the Intensive Language Program, established in 1941 by the American Council of Learned Societies. The program's underlying principle was that a sound linguistic analysis of each language should be made, followed by the elaboration of learning materials based on that analysis.

In 1943 the first courses of the Army Specialized Training Program (ASTP) were begun, and within a few months twenty-seven languages were being taught in special programs in fifty-five colleges and universities, utilizing a variety of new materials. The most outstanding of these were the manuals of the "Spoken Language" series.[2]

Moulton has listed five linguistic principles which formed the bases for these manuals and have become tenets of all audio-lingual materials:[3] (1) "Language is speech, not writing." Since language learning had traditionally been associated with reading and writing, the average American assumed that language learning and learning to read and write were two inseparable aspects of the same process. Those linguists concerned with the application of linguistics to language learning resolved, however, that the student should first learn to speak the language; reading and writing pose widely divergent problems and should

[2] Published by Holt, Rinehart and Winston.
[3] William G. Moulton, "Trends in American Linguistics: 1930–1960" in Christine Mohrmann, Alf Sommerfelt, and Joshua Whatmough, eds., *Trends in European and American Linguistics: 1930–1960* (Utrecht: Spectrum, 1961).

be undertaken only after the learner has acquired a reasonable oral proficiency. After all, the child is a relatively fluent speaker of his own native language long before he encounters reading and writing instruction in school. But since some kind of spelling system is a valuable adjunct for the adult literate learner, a system of phonemic transcription was devised to give the student a better guide to the language itself than the conventional orthography of that language. However, the student was never expected to learn to write in this system.

(2) "A language is a set of habits." The ordinary speaker is unaware of the mechanisms of speech — syntax, phonology, etc. These are produced out of an awareness of what he says and not of how he says it. Therefore, the language learner must develop his skill in the new language out of awareness. Syntactic elements, sounds, etc. must become matters of habit, and those habits may be acquired only by imitation, repetition, drill, and memorization. This process became known as "mimicry–memorization." Of course, language learning is not achieved solely by the formation of habits; it also involves the intellect, as well as the ability to perceive patterns and to analogize.

(3) "Teach the language, not about the language." Traditional methods of teaching foreign languages had required the student to learn not only the language itself, but also its codified grammar (that is, the grammatical statements or "rules" about the language) so that he could talk about the language. Linguists considered this a waste of valuable time, since grammar should never be more than a means to an end. Contrary to some misconceptions, the new materials contained a great deal of structural description, but as soon as it had served to establish the forms as matters of habit in the learner, it was no longer considered necessary to continue repeating the grammatical generalizations.

(4) "A language is what its native speakers say, not what someone thinks they ought to say." This new concept no longer allowed books (on pronunciation, grammar, etc.) to be considered as primary sources of information about a language but rather insisted that the only true source was the native speaker and established the informant as the model whom the students should imitate.

(5) "Languages are different." With this statement the linguists expressed their firm belief that traditional grammatical categories of Latin and Greek could not be applied, without distortion, to all languages. Each language should be analyzed in terms of its own grammatical structure. This ideal likewise reduced considerably the role of translation, in either direction, in language instruction. Realizing the impossibility of word-to-word equivalents in two languages, it was

deemed more valid merely to present to the student a familiar situation which he should elaborate in the foreign language, without involving the puzzle-solving obstacle of direct translation.

With these concepts, the linguists designed a system which successfully produced a practical speaking knowledge in as short a time as possible. It was never claimed that there are not other aspects of language learning, such as literature, which rightfully constitute a part of a liberal education. But the idea, evolved in these wartime courses, that grammar is a means to an end, to be learned inductively until it can be manipulated "out of awareness," is certainly a proper goal for any type of language instruction.

There is substantial agreement among the authors of today's classroom teaching materials that the initial stages of language learning must concentrate on intensive, repetitive audio-lingual practice. The ability to use and understand a language depends on the instant and accurate habitual comprehension of sounds, sentence patterns, and vocabulary. In conversation the words follow one another so rapidly that there is no time to recall and apply rules to what is being said. The student must be able to respond at once. The native speaker of the target language has, of course, acquired his language habits in childhood, through an ever-expanding and self-correcting system of imitation, correction, more imitation and more correction, analogical coinages, and vocabulary expansion. By the time he is then ten or eleven, he is in general control of all the complicated processes which our pupils must now consciously learn.[4] But the adolescent learning a foreign language outside the native country cannot duplicate the slow, natural pace of the native child. Thus, even though our teaching procedures attempt to reflect the order in which native language habits are formed, we must accomplish our task in hours instead of years, we must take into account the interference of the native language, we must teach the pupil to regain his earlier abilities to learn by ear, and we must take into account the peculiarities of the learning behavior of the age group. Obviously, only the best-informed teacher and most sophisticated materials can succeed.

Inherent in the design of such materials is the recognition of certain facts of language learning. In simplest terms, these are as follows:

First: The learner hears a new utterance. We use the term *utterance* to refer to any spoken sequence, sentence, word, or phrase.

---

[4] For more information on linguistic ontogeny (native language learning), the reader may wish to consult Charles Hockett, *A Course in Modern Linguistics* (New York: Macmillan, 1958), chapter 41.

Second: He recognizes a part of the meaning. He manages this in one of three ways: (1) he has already encountered some of its components; (2) he guesses from the context; (3) someone tells him.

Third: He grasps the meaning of the whole utterance by associating the parts with the structure that is being studied. (If he fails in this, the teacher immediately prompts him.)

Fourth: He imitates meaningfully, after the model. Continued imitation reinforces the assurance with which he utters something whose meaning is known to him. Now he must form a habit, that is, he must learn to use the newly acquired form without error. Habit calls for repetition, now guided by his own memory rather than as an echo of an outside model. Whenever his memory is imperfect, he must revert to direct imitation of the outside model before repeating further.

Fifth: As soon as repetition has made the habit secure, variation drills are introduced. Such drills vary one component or another of the model utterance to produce new expressions. Such variations explore the patterns and limits of similarity and difference tolerated by the language.

Once a reliable habit has been formed in this way, the learner will understand the model form and related utterances automatically and rapidly. The process is in no way limited to single words or idiomatic expressions, however. It is just as valid, if not more so, for the meaningful use of all grammatical forms. Of course, the internal structure of all pattern drills should be designed to encourage the student to move from the initial ability to manipulate the structure to the ultimate ability to communicate effectively using the structure.

Again, it is the work of the linguist which has made us aware of the incredible amount and kind of practice needed to make these recognitions, variations, and selections truly automatic and habitual and therefore usable. Indeed, a great part of the strategy behind the scientifically designed materials we have been discussing is to make them so efficient that there will be time in class to insure the necessary repetitions and controlled variations of the essential patterns.

As we become aware of these facts of language learning, we cannot but conclude that oral practice is the principal vehicle for the early stages of language learning. And simply from the practical point of view of time, a model utterance can be imitated and repeated far more often orally than in writing, to say nothing of its variation and correction for oral accuracy. An entire class can repeat a model many times under the immediate supervision of the teacher. Mistakes are caught on the spot and the correct form is supplied and drilled at once. The dual advantage of greater intensity in guided practice and of immediate correction makes oral practice the logical classroom procedure.

Many teachers hesitate to try an essentially oral approach for any number of reasons. Perhaps the teacher has been unable to go abroad and feels that he is not fluent enough or that his pronunciation is faulty. Perhaps he was not trained specifically as a language teacher and feels insecure in his practical control of the grammar. Perhaps he is used to a more traditional approach and feels unprepared to meet the needs of an orally conducted class. But there is no need to assume that the qualifications needed for good beginning language teaching can be acquired only through complete retraining. The function of the teacher in a beginning language class is to help the pupils acquire reliable, correct, firmly practiced habits in the language. It would be impossible, anyway, for the teacher to chat with the students at length in the foreign language about general topics before the students have learned the fundamentals of the language itself. To establish these habits, the teacher must lead the students, through intensive drill, to full control of a limited part of the foreign language which will form the foundation for their later progress.

What, then, are the *indispensable* qualifications of a competent teacher at this beginning level?

First, he serves as an oral model for his pupils' imitation. For this, he must know how to pronounce the material his students will be using and to control the structures which it contains. Part of every teacher's professional advancement depends on constantly improving that control and keeping well ahead of what is being taught in class; but no one not already a native speaker can ever achieve complete mastery of a language, and this need not be cause for discouragement, for the teacher who keeps learning is the one who best understands the problems of his students. If the teacher's own pronunciation is faulty, he must rely upon prepared tapes or discs to serve as models for his students. Although there is no real substitute for a well-trained teacher, such audio aids can always be used profitably.

Second, the teacher is the judge of his students' accuracy. He must be able to detect mistakes. His knowledge of the points of conflict between the pupils' native language habits and the structure of the foreign language (an important part of our next chapter) will help him to foresee and understand the pupils' difficulty, as well as to determine the appropriate kind and intensity of remedial practice.

Third, and finally, the teacher is a drillmaster. The textbook may provide the raw material, but conducting a successful drill is an art. To make sure that all participate, that individuals are singled out when they need to be, that the delicate balance between too much and too little is maintained are all a part of the work of an effective drillmaster.

One important aspect of the following chapters will be to examine in detail what makes for success in each of the three areas we have just mentioned.

The achievements of the approach to modern foreign language teaching we have been discussing have been impressive. In many areas of the country, professional organizations have adopted far-reaching policies establishing the audio-lingual approach as the methodological norm for schools in their zones. For example, the following declaration of philosophy adopted on November 14, 1959 by the Foreign Language Association of Northern California, summarizes that organization's commitment to many of the principles we have touched upon. It is known as the Declaration of Asilomar. While some of the language of the declaration is perhaps overly enthusiastic, it remains a worthy statement of essentially sound objectives.

I. A modern language is mainly a spoken form of communication.

II. The best way to learn a foreign language is:
   A. As to place, the country where the language is spoken.
   B. As to time, when the learner is a young child.
   C. As to method, by understanding the spoken language and speaking it before reading and writing it.

III. The best way of teaching a foreign language to those who are neither in the country in which the language is spoken nor young children is:
   A. To recreate in so far as possible the language learning environment of the foreign country.
   B. To train the learner to regain his childhood faculty of learning by ear.
   C. To train the learner to understand the spoken language and to speak it before reading and writing it.

IV. In learning a foreign language outside the foreign country, the most important single factor is the good teacher and not the language laboratory.

V. A good teacher of a foreign language speaks like a native of the foreign country and teaches by the audio-lingual method.

VI. The language laboratory serves as an aid to the teacher by intensifying the same instruction given directly by a good teacher.

Although the years since 1959 have witnessed great improvements in the techniques and materials for achieving the goals stated in the Declaration of Asilomar, we are still far from universal success in fulfilling them. Moreover, while the imperatives of the Declaration are for many teachers new and "revolutionary", no single, unified methodology has yet been devised to make of each interested and dedicated instructor an effective and efficient model of a modern language teacher.

There has always been a wide variety of methods of teaching foreign languages in the United States. Yet at no time in the history of language teaching has the profession been besieged by so many new concepts as it is today. Furthermore, public interest in foreign language education is now at a level unequalled in history. It is hardly surprising, then, that the teacher new to the field finds the task of teaching a foreign language immensely complicated.

Whether the teacher is still in training, in his first assignment, or experienced, he may have a justifiable feeling of inadequacy in preparation, which makes it difficult to function efficiently in the welter of new materials, techniques and philosophies.

For all these readers, the principal objective of this book is an orientation to today's approach,[5] although we cannot hope to exhaust the topic. We will first consider what is implied in the new methodology and then attempt to describe the application of its concepts in the teaching situation.

Landmarks in Foreign Language Teaching in the United States

1600's	Catholic missionaries taught French in New England; Spanish Jesuits taught Spanish in what is now Florida, California, and New Mexico.
1700's	German parochial schools in Pennsylvania taught German; French and German taught at academies in Philadelphia — Spanish introduced there in 1766. Latin, Greek, and Hebrew in classical curriculum in U.S. universities.
1800's	French and German predominated. Spanish strong in areas of Spanish and Mexican influence. Spanish, French, and German in universities gained acceptance beside the "classical" languages. Modern Language Association founded in 1883.

---

[5] Donald D. Walsh has suggested the term FSM, the abbreviation for Fundamental Skills Method, as a preferable substitute for "audio-lingual." He says, "We prefer it to 'audio-lingual' because this phrase can be misinterpreted as an approach of restriction to two of the four skills (listening comprehension, speaking, reading and writing). It can also be confused with official approval of one set of teaching materials (Harcourt-Brace-World's A-LM series)." "The MLA Foreign Language Program," *Hispania*, XLVIII (1965), p. 395.

Early 1900's	Universities added courses of study in wide selection of modern foreign languages.
1914–1945	German waned in popularity for political and "patriotic" reasons.
1942	Slavic languages introduced in many secondary schools.
1942–1945	Army Specialized Training Program.
1947 to present.	Growth of audio-lingual approach to foreign language teaching at all levels.
1958	National Defense Education Act.

▶ EXERCISES

1. How do the facts of language learning mentioned thus far support the view that the oral approach is the most successful vehicle for beginning language studies?
2. In what ways is the line of separation between the principal factors inherent to all intensive audio-lingual methods and the traditional methods clearly defined?
3. Which conditions existing in the traditional language program today prevent the average student from acquiring adequate audio-lingual skills in the regular four-semester high school language course? Refer whenever possible to any program in which you may teach or observe.
4. To what extent do problems inherent to the teaching of reading and writing skills make it advisable to postpone them until after the learner has acquired a reasonable oral proficiency in the language?

REFERENCE BOOKS AND ARTICLES

ANGIOLILLO, PAUL F. *Armed Forces' Foreign Language Teaching: A Critical Evaluation and Implications* (New York: S. F. Vanni, 1947).

BROOKS, NELSON. *Language and Language Learning*, 2nd ed. (New York: Harcourt, Brace and World, 1964), especially pp. 60–81.

MÉRAS, EDMOND A. *A Language Teacher's Guide*, 2nd ed. (New York: Harper and Row, 1962), pp. 1–8; 35–52.

STACK, EDWARD M. "Advances in Language Teaching in the United States," *Advances in the Teaching of Modern Languages*, Vol. I (London: Pergamon Press, 1964).

STARR, WILMARTH et al., eds. *Modern Foreign Languages and the Academically Talented Student* (Washington, D.C.: NEA, 1960).

2

Some applications of linguistics to language teaching

The fundamental-skills approach which we have been discussing is largely the product of the findings of modern linguistic analysis. For some years now it has been held that these findings should be better known by teachers of foreign languages and that these techniques should be applied more effectively in textbooks and in the classroom. To facilitate understanding of these techniques it will be worthwhile to analyze further the nature of language learning and to restate and expand some of the ideas suggested in the preceding chapter in order to explain the basis upon which the linguist was able to construct the analyses from which the new approach of teaching evolved.

It is essential that we accept as paramount the premise that language is speaking; that it is something which we do and not just something we merely think or talk about. It is a skill, and like any skill it is best learned by practice. For years our teaching, except in rare instances, has kept the student locked away from understanding by ear and from responding by tongue. We have learned a second language first as something to read, then as something to write, and if time permitted, as something to speak.

Of course, if language is communication, then the *total* communicative experience requires simultaneous use of *all* the language skills. We communicate by understanding, which comes from hearing, and by responding, which comes from speech. However, for language to be fully known and enjoyed, the printed word is vital; it provides the knowledge of the structure and background of a language and its culture.

One of the most interesting descriptions of the language learning process and a program which reflects it is that elaborated by Nelson Brooks, who suggests that any discussion of what is involved in a good program of language learning for communication (one which emphasizes the progressive development of the four language skills — comprehension, speaking, reading, and writing — in that order) may be made clearer and briefer by first listing what it does *not* include.[1]

Language learning is not the matching of an isolated word in one language with a word in another, for this is the job of the maker of dictionaries. It is not the learning of lists of names of persons and places memorized out of context, for anyone who knows geography can name places, just as anyone who knows music can name composers. But the converse of these statements is not necessarily true. Nor is language learning the memorization of x number of isolated words, since words and idiomatic expressions are truly learned only in context. It is therefore the student's first task to learn the structure of a language rather than its vocabulary. Only after a knowledge of sounds, word order, and forms is achieved should an increase in vocabulary become an important objective.

Modern approaches to language learning do not permit the student to use the mother tongue whenever he wishes; neither do they allow the student to have recourse to a printed script at all times, for separate functions of the ear and eye in language learning must be recognized. The theory that language learning improves as the number of senses involved increases does not hold true in the early stages of sound language learning.

The study of a language is not the exhaustive exploration of rules of grammar, for while such rules may be of some help to some students in understanding how the new language works, they can easily inhibit advance in the use of the new language by focusing the student's attention on the rule itself. Nor is the repetition of paradigms (verb conjugations, noun declensions, etc.) of any real value, since language in use does not contain paradigms any more than arithmetic problems contain numbers in series.

---

[1] Nelson Brooks, *Language and Language Learning*, revised ed. (New York: Harcourt, Brace and World, 1964).

No amount of talk *about* the language can replace talk *in* the language, just as no amount of discussion about the piano will enable the learner to play the instrument. The skill of the pianist is acquired only by touching the keys; the skill of the language learner comes only from the use of his tongue.

Language learning is not an attempt to decode a foreign language into English, for the foreign language is a system fully adequate for communication in its own right. A good program does not include insistence upon talk in complete sentences, for such practice violates normal communication. The most common unit of speech is the "utterance" (a thought), while a "sentence" in its formally defined sense as containing a subject and a predication, or as possessing other "essential" structural qualifications, is a creation of the printed page and not the unit utilized by word of mouth.[2] Language learning is not a prolonged series of questions and answers, for oral communication takes place only to a limited degree in this form. The most common form of communication is that of an utterance and a rejoinder (reply): "What a beautiful day!" "It certainly is!"

Effective language teaching and learning is not a solo performance by the teacher. It is important that the teacher *model* the learnings expected of the student, but he must establish student–teacher and student–student communication, and the ultimate objective has not been reached until the teacher can withdraw from the process and observe.

And finally, language learning is not the transfer of the teacher's entire knowledge to the student. The old idea of the master and his disciple is out of place, for the student comes to language class to learn to communicate in the new language at his own level of proficiency; he does not come, for the time being at least, with the idea of becoming a language teacher, a linguist, or an expert on the culture of the countries associated with the language under study.

By the listing we have made of all the things which the program of

---

[2] The "grammatical sentence" is, of course, not the only, nor necessarily the most frequent, means by which human beings communicate in speech. Most commonly, conversation involves sentence "fragments" (such as, "Good morning," "See you," "Indeed?," "Very well," "Of course," "Pardon") which are constantly being interrupted by the other speaker or revised in midstream by the original speaker himself. For purposes of linguistic analysis and for authentic dialogue construction, we need to recognize the "utterance," which we may define as a stretch of speech bounded by silence. This stretch of speech need not necessarily contain the subject and full predication of the "grammatical sentence."

A fuller discussion of utterance definition may be found in Charles Fries, *The Structure of English* (New York: Harcourt, Brace and World, 1952), pp. 23 ff.

language learning for communication is *not*, and by recalling the many earlier misconceptions about language teaching as summarized in Chapter 1, we may arrive at a rather brief statement of what it *is* and, thus, how it differs from the older approaches which we shall call "traditional." Our statement is based on broad professional agreement about objectives, methods, materials, and tests.

The major objective is to learn to understand and speak the language as it is used in its culture. In these terms, the roles of English, translation, grammar rules, and the textbook itself are reduced to very modest proportions. The cultural objective should remain, together with the literary objective, for the development of language competence cannot fail to be strengthened by the study of literature. Selected samples of good literature, in suitable amounts, are important in language study almost from the beginning in order to acquaint the learner with the characteristics which lift them above language to the level of fine art.

It is with these fundamental principles that the linguist's contribution to language teaching begins and from which the audio-lingual approach has evolved. It behooves the present-day teacher of foreign languages to be familiar with these principles, but many teachers who have conscientiously tried to understand them have been hindered in their attempts by the specialized nature of most linguistic studies; the unfamiliar themes and technical terminology make them hard to understand. It remains for us here to take a new look at some aspects of linguistics and to try to incorporate some of them into our work. We shall find that there is no need to be uneasy about linguistic science, once we have discovered that it is not so austere nor so inaccessible as it has frequently been made to seem.

"Linguistics is simply the objective, systematic analysis of the facts of language, as it is habitually used by human beings in their relationships with one another. . . . The linguistic analyst is concerned, above all, with observing what people do when they interact by means of language. . . . The linguistic analyst's task is to discover, in whatever language he is studying, as much system as there is in it, and to describe that system as effectively as he can." [3]

The linguist's attempts to analyze the target language systematically have led him to a number of conclusions which are of immense help to the teacher of foreign languages in preparing materials and in presenting and drilling them in the classroom and laboratory. The first and most important conclusion has to do with significant contrasts: significant

---

[3] "Linguistics and Language Teaching," in *Reports of the Working Committees*, 1962 Northeast Conference on the Teaching of Foreign Languages.

contrasts within the language being taught (the target language) and significant contrasts between the target language and the native language of those who are learning it (the source language).[4] Significant contrasts are the differences in the way people speak which cause their hearers to perceive different meanings.   An example of a significant contrast within Spanish would be the difference between *gato* and *rato;* the contrast between the sound represented by *g* and that represented by *r* causes the hearer or reader to perceive a difference in meaning.   In discovering significant contrasts, the linguist breaks down his material (on all levels of language structure — sounds, forms, and combinations of forms) into minimum meaningful units.   To designate these units, he uses the suffix *-eme*, added to various Greek roots:

phon- "sound"   *phoneme* "significant unit of sound"
Exemplified by the *gato/rato* contrast described above; the /*g*/ and /*r*/ are Spanish phonemes.

morph- "form"   *morpheme* "significant unit of form"
A morpheme is a stretch of speech which recurs in the language with approximately the same meaning. Thus, in English, *cats* is made up of two morphemes: *cat* and *-s*. *Cat* has an identifiable meaning and *-s* bears a definite meaning.

tagm- "arrangement"   *tagmeme* "significant unit of arrangment"
Defined in Chapter 5.

graph- "writing"   *grapheme* "significant unit of writing"
The letter *v*, for example, may be written as a capital or small letter, yet in both cases it represents the same sound.

He then couches his description of any given language in terms of the phonemes, morphemes, and tagmemes which it contains, and its writing system in terms of the graphemes which are used to represent the language.

The same technique, of course, can be applied to both the target and the source languages.   By contrasting the significant units (the "-emes") of the target language with those of the source language, the linguist will be able to isolate clearly and sharply the points at which the two languages differ.   In this way, the Spanish teacher whose pupils are native speakers of English will be able to make use of the results of such a contrastive study of Spanish and English in order to concentrate his

---

[4] Robert A. Hall Jr., *Linguistics and Your Language* (New York: Doubleday Anchor Books A–201, 1960), pp. 89–92.

attention on those points where the pupil will be more likely to transfer his English habits into Spanish.

This kind of systematic analysis is of inestimable value in language teaching. Although we must recognize that linguistics itself is not a way of learning languages, nor a method of teaching them, we must also recognize that linguistics provides the techniques which furnish the most accurate and the most efficiently formulated data upon which the teaching and learning of languages can be built. By comparing the points of contrast of the target language with those of the source language, we highlight and predict the major difficulties for the learner. We are thus able to construct, quite systematically, teaching and testing materials which will give emphasis to the points of real difficulty. Furthermore, linguistic analysis enables us to describe the language to be learned more simply and economically than is done in conventional grammars. Finally, since linguistics is concerned first with the *spoken* language, systematic analysis and drill on pronunciation problems from the beginning (not just the pronunciation of target language sounds, but intonation and phrase rhythm as well) lead students to an early and broad mastery of the spoken forms.

The language teacher and the learner gain a great number of collateral advantages through the application of linguistic principles. First, we have an answer to the old problem of "what Spanish shall we teach." The specific dialect of Spanish we teach (Castilian, Mexican, etc.) is unimportant, so long as the teacher controls it well, and the student learns it consistently. Naturally, we aim at dialects and levels of speech recognized as appropriate to educated speakers of the target language, while remaining free from regional and local biases. As we mentioned in Chapter 1, linguistics, in studying the totality of man's language behavior, has brought us to realize that his ordinary, everyday speech is fundamental, and that his more pretentious "best-behavior" speech is really based on his everyday speech. Although the study of stylistics is fascinating, it is properly the concern of advanced courses and does not really belong in elementary and intermediate work. What we must attempt to do is to introduce the beginning student to the ordinary usage of normal people in real-life situations. Our goal must be, for the initial stages, a good command of a normal, everyday variety of the language, as it is spoken by ordinary, educated people.

Another collateral realization that has come to the aid of the language teacher through linguistics is that language is not just a series of individual words which one first acquires and then learns how to put together in sentences. Rather, new lexical items are learned as parts of whole native utterances and their meanings associated with the situation in which they are used. Vocabulary lists, consequently, are useless since they present target language words with source language "equivalents," ignoring context, situation, and structure, which are the only valid means of developing both an active and passive vocabulary in the target language. The whole matter of contextual learning of vocabulary will be discussed more fully in Chapter 12.

By emphasizing the conversational nature of language, linguistics has shown that when humans speak, it is normally in sentence and dialogue form. Psychologists have shown, incidentally, that even when we "think to ourselves" we do so more often than we realize in dialogue form, either in conversation with ourselves or with an imaginary interlocutor.[5] Thus, the most economical and realistic way in which we can present new material to our students is in dialogue form, with sentences carefully constructed to reflect, as realistically as possible — considering, of course, graded grammar and vocabulary — the kind of conversation that might be heard among native speakers of the language. Exercises in formal expository prose, poetry, songs, and the like admittedly have their place, but normally not in the very beginning stages.

Up to now we have been discussing the advantages to the teacher. Linguistic principles can be useful directly to the student. Any person of high school age is mentally mature enough to make his own inferences about language structure but, unless properly guided, he has an alarming tendency to reach wrong conclusions. This imposes at least two conditions on the teacher and the textbook writer: (1) to encourage correct generalization (or induction) by making sure that the examples of a construction cover it adequately, but do not overreach it — i.e., that the "rule" will almost shine through of itself; and (2) to leave nothing to chance, but after the student has tentatively framed his own generalization to give him the right one, succinctly and accurately stated.

But aren't these "generalizations" really the same as the grammar explanations which we have always used? In the sense that they are presentations of the facts of the language, yes. The problem is that many grammatical rules do not accord with the facts of the language as it is spoken today. Many are based on usage of past centuries and many attempt to prescribe rules on the basis of an imagined cultured language which does not exist in anyone's speech. For example, in many parts of Spanish America, students are taught to use a labiodental *v* [6]

---

[5] For a general discussion of psychological principles of foreign language teaching in the modern approach, see Wilga Rivers, *The Psychologist and the Foreign Language Teacher* (Chicago: University of Chicago Press, 1964).

[6] See Chapter 4.

in words like *vaca, lavar, envío*. This is an invention of the schools (making the well-known mistake that we have already mentioned of confusing writing with speech) and has never been the habit of most speakers of Spanish, cultured or otherwise. Consequently, insisting on it is purposeless. Furthermore, the very term "grammar" has meant so many different things in the last two centuries that it really needs to be replaced or very carefully redefined. For some, "grammar" has meant an obedience to *a priori* rules, especially those based on Latin. For others, it has meant either an insistence on correct spelling or drills on paradigmatic forms. For yet others, it has meant an avoidance of supposedly socially disfavored terms, such as *ain't*.

Mostly, these meanings of "grammar" have been picked up not in foreign language classrooms but in English classes — that is, in classes where the student is being taught to "improve" his own speech and writing, to adopt a more elevated dialect of his own language. (We say this as no disparagement of the poor English teacher — she has her hands full — who, unhappily, has too often been guided by texts that teach the sins to avoid, rather than the virtues to pursue.) To the linguist, and to the foreign language teacher, "grammar" means something different: it is simply the structure of the language, and, far from throwit out of the window (as might be appropriate, sometimes, with grammar in the other senses), we ought to teach it with a vengeance, even — or especially — in the audio-lingual approach in which the student will be unable to learn without knowing the structural facts and how to manipulate them. Call the explanation of these facts grammar, structural analysis, generalizations, or anything else; what matters is that we not be misled by the traditional misconceptions of what a grammatical explanation should be.

To list here the many facts of the language which are apparent in the spoken system, but masked by orthographic conventions, would be superfluous. Let one suffice: whole areas of extremely important and meaningful speech behavior, such as stress and intonation, tend to be left out of consideration because they are only imperfectly — and sometimes not at all — indicated in the orthographic system. Yet, intonation and "tone of voice" are highly important in determining the emotional attitudes of those with whom we are conversing. Many speakers of Spanish have, from the outset, a hostile reaction toward North Americans, because the latter seem to be always overemphasizing everything they say, as when a North American says, "*¡Yó nó compréndo ló qué ustéd díce!*", or intones a question such as, "*¿Cómo se llama usted?*" with an intonation pattern typical of English but not of Spanish:

Wrong:

"¿Cómo se llama usted?"

Right:

"¿Cómo se llama usted?"

This is due to the carrying over of American English stress and intonation patterns into Spanish. Such structural features must be given our very special attention in teaching, first, because they are masked by the writing system; second, because the student is largely unaware of the intonation patterns in his native language; and, third, because few materials, except the very newest, contain drills of any kind on stress and intonation.

Until very recently, the presentation of all but the most obvious syntactic features has been hampered by the absence of an effective analytical technique. It has long been considered impossible to describe such phenomena as the position of modifiers (like *bueno*, *pobre*, and *mal[o]*) or the order of words in the sentence except in terms of some vague "affective" meanings. In the last few years, however, extensive procedures for describing syntactic structures have been developed, and, with these modern developments, there is no longer any excuse for failing to extend our grammatical treatment to the totality of the language we are teaching and to the totality of its differences from the totality of English structure.

Now, what of drills? Their main purpose is to hammer home points of structure that cause difficulty. Obviously, they must be constructed carefully with this in view and must be graded from the simple to the complex. They must also be provided in profusion since, as we saw in Chapter 1, to form a linguistic habit, to reinforce it, and finally to control it, infinite repetition is needed. The newest materials contain pattern drills of this type and in the suggested quantity. However, it is always possible to adapt and amplify existing texts by supplying new drill material, provided that whoever makes the drill material has the necessary competence.[7]

"The person doing the job must have a thorough command of three skills: he or she must know the target language itself well; must understand its structure and be able to identify the crucial points where it differs from the learner's language; and must know how to construct substitution and variation drills so that the student can practice the appropriate patterns."[8]

---

[7] See Chapter 9. [8] "Linguistics and Language Teaching," *op. cit.*, p. 16.

Chapter 5 will discuss pattern drills — what they are, how they are constituted, and how they can be used. With this information, the beginning teacher who is not a native speaker of Spanish may prepare the drills with some confidence and then seek the services of a native to make the recordings for the language laboratory. Needless to say, however, any drills created by nonnatives can always profit from inspection by a native speaker to insure naturalness.

A great deal of public and professional interest has been aroused in the fundamental skills approach by recent progress in the field of equipment, especially the language laboratory. While such interest is always helpful, there is danger that the language laboratory may be used unwisely. Bad materials are not improved by putting them on tape. One hears reports of teachers making recordings in an atrocious accent, or merely committing to tape the exercises or readings from older texts, or even reciting grammar rules. Some go to the extreme of holding classes in the language laboratory without making any use of the mechanical aids at all. As we shall see in our chapter on language laboratories, the purpose of the laboratory is pattern reinforcement and drill. Whereas many of the new texts come with drill tapes already prepared, a teacher who is obliged to continue using an old-fashioned text must know something of linguistic analysis if he is to supplement the text with well-made dialogues and drills for laboratory use.

These, then, are the principal areas in which the findings of linguistic science are indisputably of great importance. By approaching our problems with the attitude that the findings of linguistics can be understood by any intelligent person and that they can be applied to the classroom situation with great effect by any teacher with a good command of the language, we shall be able to take advantage of them to improve our teaching.

Skeleton of the First-Year Audio-Lingual Unit

Although format and procedure may vary, most of the basic audio-lingual materials provide the same types of learning activities for all students. All audio-lingual units at beginning levels consist of two main features: dialogues and pattern drills. Other kinds of learning exercises complete the unit and various mechanical devices (tapes, transparencies, films, etc.) may be employed to their fullest extent, as long as all efforts are carefully integrated with the learning objective of the moment.

    I. *Basic dialogue.* To be memorized by the student. The dialogue should represent a true-to-life situation, real and enjoyable. The language should be authentic, contemporary and informal — that which would be used in equivalent circumstances by native speakers of the same age as the learner.

A. Situational presentation, with students' books closed, to convey the meanings of the dialogue with minimal or no recourse to English translation.

B. Backward buildup with choral and individual echo of component words and phrases.

C. Use of mechanical aids to reinforce presentation.

II. *Cultural notes.*

III. *Phonetic drills.* Isolation of the most difficult problems in pronunciation which an English-speaking person will have in learning the foreign language. These drills are usually found in the teacher's manual, rather than in the student textbooks. They are necessary to offer special help and correction when pronunciation difficulties arise — as they will, since many students do not imitate the model accurately with ease.

A. In class.

B. Coordinated in the language laboratory.

IV. *Dialogue adaptation.* Relates the dialogue sentences and situation to the personal experience of the student and aids in memorization.

A. Consists of questions and answers, to be used as soon as the corresponding part of the basic dialogue has been well learned.

B. These questions and answers are varied, but only within the limits of the students' learned vocabulary and structure.

C. No new vocabulary or structure is introduced.

D. The purpose of the dialogue adaptation is to use known words and patterns in a different context and in more personal situations.

V. *Supplementary materials.* Vocabulary, idioms, and expressions (dates, weather, etc.) suggested in the basic dialogue, which may be learned and practiced easily as part of the daily routine. They are taught by repetition and learned by rote.

VI. *Grammatical (structure or pattern) drills.* Exercises which drill certain grammatical points of the language in terms of the language itself. The purpose of these drills is to present an utterance which exemplifies a particular grammatical point. They should be formulated in such a way that the items illustrating this point are varied without changing the essential structure of the utterance. Therefore, the student's attention is focused on the slot where the changes are to be made; he learns to manipulate properly the items that can be substituted in the slot, and gradually develops an awareness and understanding of the pattern he is handling. As a model for this section, we shall take examples and diagrams from the section on shortened adjectives from Bolinger *et al.*, *Modern Spanish*, pp. 146 ff.[9]

A. Identification of the point to be drilled.
B. Examples, in Spanish only, for choral and individual echo, divided into as many groups as deemed necessary by morphological considerations (tense, mood, gender, etc.).

    1. ¡Qué **buen** café es éste!
    2. Para café **bueno,** no hay como este lugar.
    3. **Buena** idea.

    4. Tuve un **mal** día.
    5. El suyo siempre tiene algo **malo.**
    6. ¡Qué **mala** cara trae!

    7. Fue un **gran** jefe.
    8. Como **gran** cosa me concedieron hasta mañana.
    9. Ayer hubo una reunión **grande.**

    10. ¿Desea dejar **algún** recado?
    11. ¿Quieres traerme **algún** buen libro?
    12. ¿**Alguno** de Uds. trajo plata?
    13. Hay que pensar en progresar **alguna** vez.

    14. **Ningún** extranjero puede.
    15. No tuvieron **ninguna** reunión.

    16. Venga **cualquier** día.
    17. ¿Cuál desea Ud.? — **Cualquiera.**

C. Extrapolation. Diagram or chart of the construction (Spanish only) to show the process involved.

---

[9] *Modern Spanish*, 2nd ed., © 1960, 1966 by Harcourt, Brace & World, Inc., and reprinted with their permission.

BEFORE SINGULAR NOUN		ELSEWHERE
Masculine	*Feminine*	
buen	buena	bueno, –a, –os, –as
mal	mala	malo, –a, –os, –as
	gran	grande, –s
algún	alguna	alguno, –a, –os, –as
ningún	ninguna	ninguno, –a, –os, –as
un	una	uno, –a, –os, –as
primer	primera	primero, –a, –os, –as
tercer	tercera	tercero, –a, –os, –as

D. Note. "Except for *grande*, the shortening takes place only in the masculine singular when the adjective precedes the noun and nothing more than another adjective intervenes."

any man	**cualquier hombre**	either one ⎱
any woman	**cualquier mujer**	any one ⎰ **cualquiera**

"The shortened form **cualquier** is used before a singular noun, either masculine or feminine. **Cualquiera** is used independently of the noun."

E. Drills. Beginning with simple substitution (item substitution) drills, then proceeding to as many variations as desired.

    1. Aquí no hay ninguna **profesora.**
       (profesor, tijeras, frijoles)

    2. ¿Desea dejar algún **recado?**
       (cosa, libros, herramientas)

    3. ¡Qué buena **carne!**
       (café, frijoles, comidas)

    4. Tuve una mala **idea.**
       (día, preguntas, exámenes)

    5. Aquí hay un **médico.**
       (planta, funcionarios, refinerías)

    6. No puedo venir la primera **semana.**
       (día, tarde, mes)

    7. ¿Dónde está el tercer **libro?**
       (noticia, documento, cuenta)

8. Es un gran **filósofo.**
(señora, jefes, profesores)

9. Déme cualquier **libro** de éstos.
(cartera, libros, pluma)

. . . .

14. No es una **señorita** cualquiera.
(señor, señoras, señores)

F. Discussion of pattern. Grammatical generalization.
G. Reinforcement drills. Generally these are not necessary, but if used, the best is the combined replacement drill.

VII. *Recombination Drills.* Brief narratives or conversations (directed dialogues, conversation stimuli) which recombine the materials of the preceding and present units in a new form. Slight variations in structure and some new vocabulary may appear.

VIII. *Readings* (in later units).
A. In written form, for reading comprehension.
B. On tape in laboratory, or in class by teacher, to check auditory comprehension.

IX. *Response drills based on readings.*
A. In written form for orthographic practice.
B. In laboratory, or in class with tape, for oral practice.

Skeleton of the Second-Year Audio-Lingual Lesson

I. *Basic sentences* (these may be sequential dialogue or selected non-sequential sentences taken from II below, depending upon the materials being used).
A. Build-up of component words and phrases
B. Basic sentences

II. *Basic reading narrative*
A. Oral presentation
1. in breath groups
2. in complete utterances
3. with spot questions with minimal answers. This is not to test the student's ability to formulate fully adequate answers, but is rather to assure that he is following the content of the oral presentation.

B. Silent reading for comprehension
C. Questions and answers
   1. oral
   2. written

III. *Structural drills*
(internal format as in first-year course)

IV. *Grammatical generalizations*

V. *Writing drills*
A. Questions and answers to II C above
B. Dictation of I B above
C. Dictation of II above
D. Expansion and transformation
   1. as specified in the text
   2. of I B above
   3. of II B above

VI. *Reading recombination* (a new narrative, recirculating the vocabulary and structure of II above)
A. Silent reading for comprehension
B. Questions and answers
   1. oral
   2. written

Skeleton of the Third-Year Audio-Lingual Lesson

I. *Basic sentences*
A. Build-up of component words and phrases
B. Basic sentences

II. *Word study*
(focusing on special problems of vocabulary, cf. Chapter 7)

III. *Basic reading narrative*
A. Oral presentation
B. Silent reading for comprehension
C. Questions and answers
   1. oral
   2. written

IV. *Structural drills*
(same internal format as in first and second years)

V. *Grammatical generalizations*

VI. *Writing drills*
   A. As specified in text
   B. Questions and answers to III C above
   C. Dictation of I B and III B above
   D. Expansion and transformation
      1. as specified in the text
      2. narrative-to-dialogue
      3. reconstruction of narrative from topical outline
      4. reconstruction of narrative from "key words"
      5. "scene setting" for dialogues

Skeleton of the Fourth-Year Audio-Lingual Lesson

   I. *Conversation for reading, generally culturally oriented*
      A. Oral exercises
      B. Written exercises

  II. *Word study*

 III. *Basic reading narrative*
      A. Oral presentation
      B. Silent reading for comprehension
      C. Exercises
         1. oral
         2. written

  IV. *Structural drills and grammatical generalizations*

   V. *Idioms with written drills*

  VI. *Writing*
      A. Controlled narrative composition
      B. Dialogue construction

▶ EXERCISES

1. Discuss the findings of linguistic science and how they are of service to language teachers, whatever method is used to teach the language.
2. Discuss how grammar, as it is presented in the audio-lingual lesson, differs considerably from the normative (prescriptive) grammar taught in the traditional classroom.
3. Discuss how an analysis of the comparative structure of the source and target languages can be of great benefit even to an experienced teacher.

4. Discuss the role of the nonnative teacher with regard to the construction of original drill materials for classroom and laboratory use.
5. Discuss why the teacher never assumes a secondary role in an audio-lingual course.
6. Discuss to what degree a teacher accustomed to teaching methods we have characterized as inadequate will have to change in converting to the fundamental skills approach.
7. Discuss why the "generalization" presented in an audio-lingual lesson is not superfluous even though the "extrapolation" has already presented the structure being drilled.
8. Discuss why the teacher should never introduce a vocabulary list to accompany an audio-lingual lesson.
9. Discuss the advantages and disadvantages of the fact that in beginning audio-lingual lessons the students' responses are closely controlled.

REFERENCE BOOKS AND ARTICLES

ALLEN, HAROLD B., ed. *Readings in Applied English Linguistics* (New York: Appleton-Century-Crofts, 1958).

ANDERSSON, THEODORE, ed. *The Teaching of Modern Languages* (New York: UNESCO, 1955).

BLOCH, BERNARD and GEORGE TRAGER. *An Outline of Linguistic Analysis* (Baltimore: Linguistic Society of America, 1942).

BLOOMFIELD, LEONARD. *Outline Guide for the Practical Study of Foreign Languages* (Baltimore: Waverly Press, 1942).

BOLINGER, DWIGHT L. "Are We Playing Fair With Our Students Linguistically?" (*Hispania* XXXIV, 1951), 131–136.

CÁRDENAS, DANIEL N. "The Application of Linguistics in the Teaching of Spanish" (*Hispania* XL, 1957), 456–460.

DESBERG, DAN. "Structural Linguistics and High School Language Teaching" (*Classical Outlook* XXXVII, No. 2, 1959), 13–14.

EATON, ESTHER and LYNNE NORTON. *Source Materials for Secondary School Teachers of Foreign Languages* (Washington, D.C.: USOE, 1962).

HADEN, ERNEST F. "Descriptive Linguistics in the Teaching of a Foreign Language" (*Modern Language Journal* XXIX, 1954), 170–176.

HILL, ARCHIBALD A. "Language Analysis and Language Teaching" (*Modern Language Journal* XL, 1956), 335–345.

HOCKETT, CHARLES F. "Objectives and Processes of Language Instruction" (*California Schools* XXX, 1959), 112–116.

JOHNSTON, MARJORIE C., ed. *Modern Foreign Languages in the High School* (Washington, D.C.: USOE, 1960).

LADO, ROBERT. *Language Teaching: A Scientific Approach* (New York: McGraw-Hill, 1964).

MACKEY, W. F. *Language Teaching Analysis* (London: Longmans, Green, 1964).

MOULTON, WILLIAM. *A Linguistic Guide to Language Learning* (New York: MLA, 1966).

NEWMARK, MAXIM, ed. *Twentieth Century Language Teaching* (New York: Philosophical Library, 1948).

NOSTRAND, HOWARD L. *et al. Research on Language Teaching: An Annotated International Bibliography for 1945–1964* (Seattle: University of Washington, 1966).

OLLMANN, MARY J., ed. *Selective List of Materials* (New York: MLA, 1962).

ORNSTEIN, JACOB. "Structurally Oriented Texts and Teaching Methods Since World War II: A Survey and Appraisal" (*Modern Language Journal* XL, 1956), 213–222.

PARKER, WILLIAM R. *The National Interest and Foreign Languages* (New York: MLA, 1965).

POLITZER, ROBERT L. *Language Learning* (Englewood Cliffs: Prentice-Hall, 1965).

RIVERS, WILGA M. *The Psychologist and the Foreign Language Teacher* (Chicago: University of Chicago Press, 1964).

ROUCEK, JOSEPH S. *The Study of Foreign Language* (New York: Philosophical Library, 1968).

WALSH, DONALD D. *What's What — A List of Useful Terms for the Teacher of Modern Languages* (New York: MLA, 1964).

Although there are many books currently available which are advertised as audio-lingual in approach, the teacher must examine carefully a wide variety of such texts before deciding which will best suit the needs of the program in which he teaches. Below are some better-known audio-lingual texts. Asterisked entries have sequential follow-up texts for second year (and, in some cases, beyond).

* AGARD, FREDERICK B. *et al. Modern Approach to Spanish* (New York: Holt, Rinehart, and Winston, 1964).

——. *Speaking and Writing Spanish* (New York: Holt, Rinehart, and Winston, 1951).

BOLINGER, DWIGHT L. *et al. Modern Spanish*, 2d ed. (New York: Harcourt, Brace and World, 1965).

* BOWEN, J. DONALD and R. P. STOCKWELL. *Foreign Service Institute Basic Spanish* (Washington, D.C.: Government Printing Office, 1961).

* HANSEN, TERRENCE and ERNEST WILKINS. *Español a lo vivo* (Waltham, Mass.: Blaisdell, 1964).

LADO, ROBERT and EDWARD BLANSITT. *Contemporary Spanish* (New York: McGraw-Hill, 1967).

* LaGRONE, GREGORY *et al. Español: Entender y hablar* (New York: Holt, Rinehart, and Winston, 1964).

* MICHALSKI, CHARLES. *Spanish: Oral Approach* (Boston: Ginn and Co., 1965).

* MUELLER, KLAUS *et al. Spanish for Secondary Schools* (Boston: D. C. Heath and Co., 1962).

* STAUBACH, CHARLES and J. W. WALSH. *First Year Spanish,* revised (Boston: Ginn and Co., 1961).

* THOMPSON, MARY P. *et al. A-LM Spanish* (New York: Harcourt, Brace and World, 1961).

3

The spoken basis of audio-lingual teaching procedures

Now that we have examined briefly the scope and form of the audio-lingual approach at its theoretical level, let us look more closely into the organization of representative audio-lingual materials and see how these theoretical concepts are put to work.

Central to the teaching of the spoken language is a principle known as "guided imitation." Some teachers prefer to call it the "mim-mem" method, referring to mimicking the model and then memorizing the pattern. Like so many of the basic concepts of the fundamental skills method, guided imitation may appear to be new but it has actually been known to teachers for many years. Certain European language teaching centers discovered its value in the nineteenth century. Its goal, like that of all audio-lingual techniques, is to teach one to speak easily, fluently, with very little nonnative accent, and to do all of this without conscious effort.

The success of the guided imitation technique depends to a very large extent upon the students' learning a relatively small body of material so well that it requires very little effort to produce it. This is what happens when one learns to speak one's own language, and this is the goal of the learner of a second language. The process is familiar to us from our education courses and is known as overlearning. It is axiomatic that, if a student overlearns every dialogue and drill as he moves through the course, he will almost certainly progress rapidly. The success of the technique also depends upon the student's attention to *exact* imitation of the model. His goal is to manipulate the sounds, sequences, and patterns of the language as accurately as possible. This implies a great responsibility for the teacher: the model that the student imitates must be a model of Spanish as people really speak it in actual conversations. Besides, the teacher must know how to guide and correct the student as he learns to imitate accurately. Above all, the normal tempo of speech must be the classroom standard; slowing down is, for our purposes, distortion.

The teacher must, therefore, be confident that what he presents to the class is a model of standard conversational Spanish. If the teacher is not confident of the excellence of his Spanish, he should, out of fairness to the students, make use of the tape recorder. Many of the latest audio-lingual texts, such as *Modern Spanish, A-LM, Entender y hablar, Español a lo vivo,* and others, come with sets of tapes containing all the exercise materials recorded under careful supervision by native speakers. Most modern tape recorders come equipped with manual or pedal on-off and reverse switches at the end of a control wire. Thus, the teacher can start and stop the tape as he moves about the room. In this way, the students imitate an accurate model but at the same time profit from the immediate correction and suggestion of the teacher if they fail to imitate the model accurately. We must repeat that there is no real substitute for the fluent teacher, but it is always wiser to use the tape model if one's own pronunciation is doubtful.

The guided imitation technique has been developed to the point (notably by the Foreign Service Institute, in Washington, D.C., where the emphasis is on fluency in the shortest possible time) of being useful in presenting materials as advanced as those which would be used in the fourth year of high school Spanish.

In almost all audio-lingual materials, the very first lessons are devoted to pronunciation problems. Drills on other aspects of the language are postponed deliberately because of the importance of developing good pronunciation habits from the very beginning. Pronunciation control is the only, the *only*, basis of real fluency. We now know that a person is readily able to understand anything that he can meaningfully say himself, provided that the correlation between the way he hears it and the way he says it is reasonably close. But we must also emphasize that pronunciation practice never ceases to be a primary concern of the language teacher. Every drill, no matter what structural point may be at issue, is also a drill on pronunciation. In short, at every step of the way, from the first year to the fourth, the teacher must be alert to faulty pronunciation habits.

The student's model for all pronunciation is the teacher, or the tape. The basic classroom procedure for learning new material according to the fundamental skills method is by direct and immediate imitation of the model. Depending upon the type of drill (and we shall look into the various types in Chapter 5), the repetition technique will vary. The most commonly used repetition technique is: teacher, students-in-chorus, teacher, individual student, teacher. The basic formula may be varied, but inherent in all repetition techniques are two axioms. First, no student is asked to imitate another. If an imitation drill is in progress, the teacher must repeat the model for each student. If he does not, the students rely upon each other as a model and mistakes are compounded as students recite one after the other. If the student is being called upon to respond with an entire phrase to a cue of perhaps one word, then, of course, he himself generates his own phrase on the basis of what he has been taught. Second, after each corrected response to either an imitation drill or a cued response drill, the teacher should repeat the correct phrase so that the student who has recited can compare his imitation or answer with the authoritative model and so that the entire class (in chorus) can have an opportunity to practice each response. The purpose in having the class imitate new items in chorus before individuals are singled out is to minimize the negative influence of nervousness or the desire not to make a mistake. The choral repetition permits individual students to have a "dry run" before they are called on to perform individually.

Although we will discuss drills at greater length in Chapter 5, it would be wise to mention here that part of a successful drill is the rhythmic manner in which it is conducted. Corrections during drills should be limited to supplying the correct form and carrying on. Detailed corrections which imply structural generalizations or special drill should be postponed until after the drill in progress has terminated.

Also within the scope of remarks on rapid drills is the question of how to indicate whether students are to respond in chorus or individually. This means the learning of a set of unmistakable gestures is necessary for the teacher and the students. Some suggested gestures will be discussed later in this chapter.

One of the problems inherent in the use of gestures stems from the size of the classroom and the arrangment of the seats. The ideal arrangement of the language classroom is that in which the seats are placed in a horseshoe fashion with the seats in the second and third rows slightly elevated. This is not possible in many cases, of course; therefore, the teacher must move about the room or station himself in a place where his movements may be seen clearly by all students.

For large classes particularly, calling the student by name to recite may be impractical, since any hesitation on the part of the teacher breaks the rhythm of the exercise. Some teachers have suggested a number system, but others reject it either because they have no specific seating plan or because they feel it is too impersonal.

The use of gesture may be impeded by a large and heavy textbook which cannot be carried easily in one hand, leaving the other free for gesture. Some teachers use a portable music stand which holds the book firmly in place and leaves both hands free for cueing. The stand can be placed in the center or at the side of the class, whichever cuts to a minimum the distance between the teacher and the farthest corner of the room. Often, however, the teacher remains "anchored" to the stand. Perhaps the best suggestion is that the teacher write the exercises for the day on 3 x 5 cards. These may be handled easily, allow the teacher to move about the room, and may be held in the hand during gestures. Some modern texts include such preprinted cards among the materials distributed with the teacher's manual.

All imitative drill is easier for younger children than for older ones. If a person is fortunate enough to have begun his study of a second language before the age of eight or ten, the powers of imitation are normally sufficient to insure excellent results in pronunciation without resorting to technical explanations of what happens to various parts of the vocal apparatus. Most older children and adults require more specific guidance based on the awareness of the particular problems in producing particular sounds. Therefore the first drills and explanations regarding pronunciation are devoted to the specific problems an English speaker with his English habits of pronunciation will have in accurately imitating the sounds and sequences of sounds in Spanish.

Speakers of English are, as a group, highly literate: that is, they are used to thinking of language, erroneously, as a written form. If it were not for this characteristic, it might be possible to teach effectively without reference to any written symbolization. Most students, however, are more comfortable when there is some kind of visual representation of what they are imitating. There is, of course, the traditional writing system which Spanish uses. As these systems go, Spanish is quite adequate for providing visual cues for persons who already speak the language. For the learner, however, many problems result. First, Spanish uses a variety of symbols (*c, s,* and *z*) to represent the sound /s/, but there is no orthographic distinction between the /z/ sound in *esgrimir* and the /s/ sound in *esclavo*. The letters *b* and *v* are especially confusing, since at the beginning of a breath group both represent an occlusive *b*, whereas between vowels they both represent a fricative *b*.

There are many, many more such examples which might be cited here. Suffice the foregoing to establish the point that the standard spelling system of Spanish is apt to be quite confusing to the beginning learner. The reason is that first, it does not adhere to a sufficiently strict principle of one symbol for each sound. Second, the student quite easily pronounces a letter such as *d* in Spanish the same way he does in English, resulting in a faulty accent. To minimize the probability of such errors, many of the newest materials make use of a device known as "respelling." The purpose of respelling is to achieve a one-to-one correspondence between the sounds of the language and the written symbols that represent them, for example [b] to represent the breath-group initial letters *b* and *v*, and [ɓ] to represent the intervocalic *b* and *v*. But wouldn't a student still pronounce the "respelled" *b* like *b* in English? Yes, he might. The only way to avoid any possibility of transfer would be to use a respelling which had nothing whatever in common with the English alphabet. Some phoneticians have adopted this idea, believing that the very unfamiliarity of the symbols is a healthy reminder that none of the English sounds is an exact duplicate of the Spanish sounds to be mastered.

Respelled symbols are not strictly a phonemic transcription but are a pedagogical device which is arrived at by comparing the sound systems of the source and target languages and then modifying the transcription through classroom experience.

In any case, most of the new audio-lingual materials use the principle of respelling to some degree in their presentation. Some texts use the phonetic respelling throughout (such as the Foreign Service Institute course and the Agard *et al.* book), while others prefer to limit it to the very first lesson or two.[1]

Another of the advantages of the phonetic respelling arrangement is that important phonological features which are almost universally neglected but which are of vital importance in achieving a near-native accent, such as intonation, can be shown. Intonation patterns can be indicated graphically by a variety of methods, among which are the following.

1. A musical staff with musical notes or dots on it:

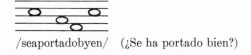

/seaportadobyen/   (¿Se ha portado bien?)

---

[1] J. D. Bowen and R. P. Stockwell, *Patterns of Spanish Pronunciation* (Chicago: University of Chicago Press, 1960). See also the same authors' "Orthography and Respelling in Teaching Spanish" (*Hispania* XL, 1957, pp. 200–205).

2. A series of dots or "accent marks" written at varying heights above the written line:

/seaportadobyen/

3. An ascending and descending wavy line described above the phrase:

/seaportadobyen/

4. A "block" line above the written phrase:

/seaportadobyen/

5. A series of numbers written slightly above the written phrase:

2   1 1   2
/seaportadobyen/

Another immediate advantage of the respelling system is that its symbolization will allow for a consistent interpretation of the pronunciation of any dialect area of the Spanish-speaking world. For example, we may teach that the respelled symbol /s/ is to be interpreted as the [s] in Spanish America or as the [θ] in Central Spain. Many regional features of pronunciation can be marked similarly.

The acquisition of a good pronunciation is, first of all, the result of careful listening and imitation, plus whatever help can be obtained from initial pronunciation drills and description, as well as from the respelling devices.

The typical (although by no means only) organization of an audio-lingual lesson, in most current materials, is as described at the end of the last chapter, beginning with a basic situational dialogue with a few pertinent notes. You will notice that any notes are relegated to a position where they do not distract the students' attention from the dialogue itself. Most of the notes are of a cultural nature. This is followed by material basically devoted to phonological and grammatical drills (also called pattern drills) and discussion. Discussion, in this sense, as we shall soon see, means a particular type of grammatical explanation (sometimes also called generalization) which follows the exercises. It is important to note, however, that discussion always *follows* the exercises, and students are not expected to generalize until after they have mastered the pattern. The sections are generally concluded by a set of drills or narratives which put together the same material as originally appeared in the basic dialogues and drills, but in a slightly different way. Readings are introduced as a part of each lesson about one-third of the way through the complete course.

The real core or heart of each unit is the basic dialogue. At best, these dialogues are re-creations of real situations a student is likely to encounter, and the vocabulary and sentences are those he is likely to need. They are written in the most authentic manner possible. While most texts grade the dialogues progressively throughout the course, others simply ask natives to prepare them without regard for the progressive difficulty of the material. Since only certain focuses are drilled in each unit, these unedited dialogues simply footnote a form which is not to be drilled. They have achieved a certain success. Some texts like to keep a continuing train of thought throughout the course. The Foreign Service Institute book sets its dialogues in a mythical South American country called "Surlandia," which is described as a "typical" Latin American country, insofar as it is possible to extract common features from among the various Latin American republics. Since their course is designed for Foreign Service personnel, as much cultural information as is practical is included in the dialogue materials. A similar program has been adopted in *Modern Spanish*, but with the focus on the American high school or college student who is travelling abroad.

At first, all new vocabulary and constructions are introduced in the basic dialogue. Later on, new items may be introduced in the drill sections, but only when it is either not the focus of the exercise or when its meaning is obvious, as in the case of cognates. Some audio-lingual texts emphasize the new items in the dialogue by isolating them for repetition before the actual phrase in which they are used; for example:

pass (to pass, to hand)	*pase (pasar)*
pass me	*páseme*
the book	*el libro*
Pass me the book.	*Páseme el libro.*

This practice is no longer as common as it once was, however, and most newer texts rely upon the backward buildup technique with the utterances of the dialogue itself to accomplish this same purpose. More will be said about this technique on page 39.

It is impractical to introduce each new word or construction more than once, so the student must be cautioned to master them as they occur. Since the drill material of each lesson is based on the dialogue, a student's failure to master the dialogue will inevitably result in poor performance in the exercises. In most of the new materials, pains have been taken to see that each word introduced will reappear many times later in the course, to help the student assimilate it in a variety of contexts.

Should these words be learned by memory at the outset? Yes, but always in context. It can be important for the student to learn the literal meaning of certain items, but such literal learning should always be followed by learning the meaning of the form in following context. The student should not be concerned if the meaning in context is strikingly different from the literal meaning. In the new materials, the teacher must bear in mind that the dialogue was prepared in Spanish. The English is simply a *post hoc* equivalent and not a literal translation. The sooner the student is made aware that the English and Spanish will not necessarily "follow" one another, the better.

The basic dialogue is commonly printed in the textbook. As we shall see later on, this simple fact has proved to be the largest single detriment to the correct learning of the dialogue. The four most common formats in which these dialogues are laid out on the pages of the textbook are: (1) in two parallel columns, Spanish orthography on the one side and English on the other; (2) back-to-back, with Spanish on the recto and English on the verso; (3) Spanish only in the lesson, English for all the dialogues as an appendix at the rear of the book; and (4) in three parallel columns, Spanish on the left, phonetic transcription in the middle, and English on the right.

All four concepts share two immense and immediate drawbacks. First, the presence of standard Spanish orthography is detrimental, as we have seen earlier in this chapter. Second, the availability of an English translation is a negative feature, be the translation on the same page or at some distance from the Spanish. Sooner or later, the classic problem of "translation" vs. "equivalent" will succeed in complicating the process of learning the dialogue. One example will illustrate this point: *La mesa está servida* is announced. The English "translation" would be: "The table is served," which makes no sense. The English "equivalent" would read: "Lunch (dinner) is ready," which makes excellent sense, except that the student will associate the Spanish and English word-by-word: *La* (the) *mesa* (lunch) *está* (is) *servida* (ready), and then risk incorrect analogical formations such as *Estoy servido* for "I am ready."

The fourth method of printing out the dialogue may be applauded as a means of retaining a visual *aide-mémoire*, without resorting to the standard orthography, yet many students experience difficulties in learning the transcription and thus a new impediment is introduced at a moment when it can least be afforded.

Much of the success of any basic dialogue depends upon the mode of presentation. It becomes a significant learning experience only when it serves to build in the pupils a sense of immediate and automatic target language responses to target language or environmental stimuli. This vital function of the basic dialogue is vitiated or even completely negated by the indiscriminate use of translation. Even though "idiomatic" translations (or "equivalents") of the dialogue lines appear either on the same page as the target language version or on the verso of that page, all indications are against its use in the initial presentation-memorization phase. Since there is no such thing as an exact translation, and since our goal is to build target language responses to real stimuli without the intermediate step of translation, it is wiser to eschew the use of English in dialogue presentation except as indicated below.

I. First, the books are taken from the students; they will not see them again until the dialogue learning sequence is complete, perhaps as much as four or five days later. The teacher then describes what the dialogue is about. This description may be done in English or in the target language. It is a short prose summary in which visual aids and realia are used extensively. The purpose of this initial description is to make certain that the pupils understand the context in which the dialogue is to take place. Perhaps this initial description will have to be repeated; perhaps the teacher will wish to ask a question or two of individual students to ascertain whether the description is clearly in mind, even when done in English.

II. Now we are ready to model the dialogue itself. Referring to the same visual aids and realia as in I above, in order to recall the context as vividly as possible, the teacher reads the dialogue (target language only). Three complete readings usually suffice. Then students are called to the front of the room and, as the teacher repeats the dialogue (target language only), the selected students "walk through" the parts being read. They do not speak. After this has been done two or three times, the students return to their seats and all listen to the dialogue yet once again.

III. Now that the situation is clear, the teacher begins the modelling of the dialogue for choral and individual repetition, using backward buildup where indicated, making articulatory corrections of mispronunciations.

IV. Additional repetitions of the dialogue now follow, with the class involved in role playing: (1) the teacher does the first line, the class in chorus does the second, etc.; (2) then the roles are reversed; (3) the same procedure, dividing the class in half and having the first half do the first line, then the second half do the second, etc.; or the teacher does the first line and an individual student the second, then the teacher does the third and another individual student the fourth, etc. There are numerous other variations of this step.

V. Once the dialogue sequence has reached this point, the students are sent to the language laboratory (or home with the take-home records) to memorize the dialogue. Again, they operate without the book. Only oral stimuli are yet permitted.

VI. After the students have memorized the dialogue, the next class, or a portion thereof, is devoted to checking their performance.

Visual aids are referred to from the beginning. In some cases these will be pen-and-ink drawings of a rough nature done by the teacher himself. In others, they will be the printed charts that sometimes accompany the textbook in use. In yet others, they will be color drawings or magazine clippings collected by the teacher.

The following procedures for performing step III of the above outline have been used with considerable success:

A. *Modelling.* It is suggested that the teacher model the line three times before calling for any choral echo. He must use the same speed and intonation as the speaker on the tape (if the tapes are not available and the teacher is not certain of the intonation, he should consult a native speaker), and free use should be made of authentic kinesics (facial expression, body movements, etc.) and the visual aids to recall meanings established earlier. The gesture suggested to indicate that the students are only to listen is that of the arms extended, with palms of the hands facing the students.

B. *Backward buildup.* Prior to the class the teacher has analyzed the line and has divided it into logical utterances, thought groups, and intonation patterns. As an example, let us take the first line of the dialogue in *A-LM*, Unit 8: *Tú eres de la Argentina, ¿verdad, Domingo?* This line would be divided: *Tú eres / de la Argentina / ¿verdad, Domingo?*

For backward buildup on this line the teacher will model *¿verdad, Domingo?* with proper intonation, two or three times, then elicit choral repetition an equal number of times, always repeating the utterances between the choral echoes. The gesture to indicate that the entire group is to echo is the sign commonly used for "come here," done slowly with both hands. Choral response is continued until no blatant pronunciation errors are heard. Then, using the same gesture, with only one hand, the teacher indicates several different individuals who should echo the utterance. It must *always* be modelled by the teacher between the individual echoes, just as it was between the choral echoes.

The learning of this line will be completed with two more steps, in which the procedures outlined above are used, first with the phrase *de la Argentina, ¿verdad, Domingo?* and finally with *Tú eres de la Argentina, ¿verdad, Domingo?* The same procedure is used in presenting the second line. When this has been mastered, the teacher returns to drill the first two lines together, then adds the third for thorough drill, returns to drill the first three lines together, adds the fourth, and so on.

Correction in pronunciation is never made by stopping the individual student and insisting that he repeat until he has mastered it. If a student pronounces incorrectly, the teacher immediately models the utterance, calls for full choral echo, models it again, proceeds to another student for individual echo, models it again, and then returns to the student who made the original error.

Of course, some students have less success at perfecting their pronunciation purely by imitation. For these students, the technique of articulatory correction is recommended and will be discussed in greater detail in Chapter 4.

The merit of the backward buildup technique lies in the fact that the oral memory is considerably shorter than the visual memory. That is, if a learner is attempting to memorize a line of some length given orally, he tends to remember what he heard first and to forget what he heard last. Therefore, once the entire line has been modelled, the emphasis for repetition should begin on the utterance with which the line concludes and slowly build backwards. This method also serves to strengthen correct intonation, for the teacher is always modelling each phrase with the intonation which it has in that sentence, no matter how strange it may seem when isolated.

A number of other techniques have proven highly successful in reinforcing the learning of the dialogue and in adding variety and interest. These may be introduced as soon as two or three lines of the dialogue have been thoroughly presented as indicated above.

1. **Role playing: teacher-class.** The teacher gives the first line, the students in chorus add the second, which the teacher immediately models. The teacher then proceeds to the third line, the students give the fourth, which the teacher models, etc. It is

important that the roles be reversed in this process so that the class has the opportunity to say each line several times.

2. **Role playing: class only.** One half of the class, or some indicated group (such as all the girls or all the boys), gives the first line, which the teacher models, followed by the next line given in chorus by the other group. Reversing roles is also necessary in this procedure.

3. **Role playing: teacher–individual student.** The teacher plays one role and asks different students to add the next line. The teacher will always model the rejoinder of the student and elicit, by gesture, full choral echo when errors have been made.

4. **Role playing: students.** Roles played by individual students, with teacher modeling after each student performance and calling for full choral echo when necessary.

5. **Chain drills.** The teacher starts the dialogue and proceeds around the class with each successive student adding the next line. For variety the teacher may start the dialogue and then, by gesture (in this case, merely pointing), indicate students, not in their order of seating, to give the next line.

While it is necessary to follow the vertical sequence of the dialogue in the early stages of its learning, it is worthwhile to introduce a different technique involving horizontal learning once the students have a reasonable command of the material. That is, the teacher gives line 3, let us say, and the student is to respond with line 4. This avoids the danger of the student feeling that he can only give line 4 if he has heard the dialogue from the beginning, as he memorized it, just as the student who has been forced to memorize and drill verb paradigms finds it difficult to produce the form *habló* unless he first thinks or says to himself *hablé, hablaste*, the two preceding forms in the paradigm.

This horizontal concept may also be used in the chain drills. That is, the first student gives any line he chooses, and the next must give the appropriate rejoinder. The third student then gives any line he chooses and the following line must be given by the next student. Of course, the teacher will always model each line and each response after the students give them.

The amount of repetition necessary will depend on the length of the utterance and the difficulty of pronunciation involved. It is absolutely essential that the teacher follow the text of the dialogue religiously, or better yet, that he memorize the dialogue beforehand so that he will never deviate from his "score" and thus add confusion to the procedure. The value of having the dialogue written on 3 x 5 cards for teacher use (which do not obstruct the system of gestures) has been mentioned earlier.

Once the teacher has presented the dialogue, utilizing the above procedures, the student is told that he must now memorize the dialogue, or a portion of it, as his homework. He may take advantage of the language laboratory for drill with the tapes, or he may practice at home with the take-home records. If the text is accompanied by such records, the students may be asked to purchase them, or in some instances, the school may have a supply of the records which are made available to the students for home study through a library system.

If the school has not provided a language laboratory, it is suggested that the various teachers take their turn at staying in their rooms one half-hour after school, with a tape recorder which is available to the students. Most modern texts are accompanied by tapes which may be purchased or borrowed from the publisher for duplicating purposes. If none are available by these means, then the teacher should have a native colleague in the school or district make the necessary tapes.

After the students have memorized the dialogue, the next class may be devoted to checking their performance on the materials in one or all of the following ways: (1) having students stand before the class, or at their seats, facing each other, and present the dialogue as a living situation, (2) using the chain drills discussed earlier, or (3) utilizing the directed dialogue drills provided in many texts. If these dialogues are committed perfectly to rote memory, the following drills will go easily and rapidly and produce the best results. As much as half the time available for a given unit can be invested in perfecting the basic dialogue without distorting the presentation of the unit.

Two other techniques are frequently used but are not recommended: (1) eliciting a written response, or (2) reproducing the dialogue by giving cues in English, which is indeed the easiest and fastest way of checking. Both of these, however, fail to accord with the concepts of skill separation and perception of meaning without recourse to English. Neither of these is necessary if the dialogue has been presented as outlined above, although many teachers find that combining one or another of these techniques with those described above is profitable.

Once the entire dialogue has been memorized from oral stimuli, the textbooks are returned to the students and they are permitted to see the printed text. The use of the dialogues in learning reading and writing will be discussed in a later chapter.

The basic dialogue is followed by drills. Patterns of the structure of the language which have been learned in the basic dialogues are expanded and manipulated in the drills. In Chapter 5 we will come to meet a variety of drill types. Most, varied as they may be with regard to format, focus either on the systematic variation of selected basic sentences within the structure and vocabulary the student has already learned, or on the structure of the language, to provide a systematic coverage of all important patterns.

All drills are planned to be answered rapidly. They are best done orally with only the teacher's book open, although some, because of their complicated nature, may be done with the students' books open. Generally, the manner of presenting the drill is obvious from the format of the text. Sometimes, however, the teacher will be wise to do a "pre-run" at home before presenting the drill in class. Some texts provide the answers to drills for the teacher's convenience and for the student to refer to when studying outside of class. Generally, if a drill is found to be hard, it is because the student did not adequately master the dialogue and possibly also the preceding drills. Audio-lingual drills reject any similarity to mathematical drills in that they are not to be puzzled out. The emphasis is on doing them rather than on figuring them out. They do not contain tricks and they are not intended as tests (although some may be used as such after they have been done in class).

After the drills themselves, there is a more detailed discussion of the pattern. These descriptions are written in a condensed and somewhat technical fashion. In some materials these are called grammatical explanations; others prefer the terms generalizations, descriptions, discussions, etc. An effort is always made to keep these explanations accessible, clear, and readable. But it must be recognized that a description of a language is a technical sort of thing, and simplification is attained only by sacrificing comprehensiveness and accuracy. The student is actually acquiring through these discussions a set of analytical tools which should serve him through the balance of his career as a language learner. Therefore, our goal is always to present explanations which will not need to be revised at each step of development.

Later units have conversation and reading selections, as we have mentioned. The conversation part is designed to help the student bridge the gap between the more or less mechanical stimulus-response activity of the drills and the skill of free conversation, which is the ultimate aim of the audio-lingual course. These so-called recombinations extend the abilities of the student into ever more natural situations. The recombination narratives are usually of an anecdotal type, or a description of an event or situation which is sometimes further recast as a directed dialogue in which the teacher acts as a prompter for students who take the various parts as actors. The prompter gradually withdraws his help so that in the end the conversation is carried on freely.

Reading selections are designed in most new materials to provide interesting information about the culture of the Spanish-speaking peoples. At the outset, these reading selections do not present words or structures that the student has not already met in the dialogues and drills. About halfway through the course, however, reading selections may be used to expand the students' vocabularies.

▶ EXERCISES

1. Since the students will seldom have the opportunity in real-life conversation to use the *exact* lines of any dialogue given in an audio-lingual lesson, why is it essential that these dialogues be memorized perfectly?
2. Since intensive choral response can become monotonous for the students and provide no opportunity for the teacher to hear individual errors, should it be kept to a minimum in the audio-lingual lesson?
3. Can the judicious use of the tape recorder in the classroom make modelling by the teacher unnecessary?
4. Is the use of pictorial aids in presenting the dialogues useful only to those teachers whose histrionic abilities do not permit them to present the material effectively without the aids?
5. Does the method of correcting students' errors suggested in this chapter have any intrinsic value? Is it based on sound principles of language learning?
6. Can the teacher who is not provided with a language laboratory or portable tape or disc recorders expect to teach effectively in the fundamental skills approach?
7. Does the organization of the audio-lingual lesson correspond to the principles of language learning outlined in Chapters 1 and 2?

REFERENCE BOOKS AND ARTICLES

BANATHY, BELA *et al.* "The Use of Contrastive Data in Foreign Language Course Development," in Albert Valdman, ed., *Trends in Language Teaching* (New York: McGraw-Hill, 1965).

Curricular Change in the Foreign Languages. 1963 Colloquium on Curricular Change (Princeton: College Entrance Examination Boards, 1963).

FERGUSON, CHARLES, ed. *Linguistic Reading Lists for Teachers of Modern Languages* (Washington, D.C.: Center for Applied Linguistics, 1963).

GAGE, WILLIAM W. *Contrastive Studies in Linguistics: A Bibliographical Checklist* (Washington, D.C.: Center for Applied Linguistics, 1961).

HALL, PAULINE C. *A Bibliography of Spanish Linguistics* (Baltimore: Waverly Press, 1956).

HALL, JR., ROBERT A. *Introductory Linguistics* (Philadelphia: Chilton, 1964).

HAMMER, JOHN H., ed. *A Bibliography of Contrastive Linguistics* (Washington, D.C.: Center for Applied Linguistics, 1965).

HILL, ARCHIBALD A. "Language Analysis and Language Teaching" (*Modern Language Journal* XL, 1956), 335–345.

LADO, ROBERT. *Linguistics Across Cultures* (Ann Arbor: University of Michigan Press, 1957).

———. "Linguistics and Foreign Language Teaching" (*Language Learning* X, 1961), 29–41.

MOULTON, WILLIAM G. *A Linguistic Guide to Language Learning* (New York: MLA, 1966).

———. "Applied Linguistics in the Classroom" (*PMLA* LXXVI, 1961), 1–6.

ORNSTEIN, JACOB and WILLIAM GAGE. *The ABC's of Languages and Linguistics* (Philadelphia: Chilton, 1964).

POLITZER, ROBERT L. "The Impact of Linguistics on Language Teaching: Past, Present and Future" (*Modern Language Journal* XLVIII, No. 3, 1964), 146–151.

POLITZER, ROBERT L. and CHARLES N. STAUBACH. *Teaching Spanish: A Linguistic Orientation,* revised ed. (Boston: Blaisdell, 1965).

RICE, FRANK and ALLENE GUSS, eds. *Information Sources in Linguistics* (Washington, D.C.: Center for Applied Linguistics, 1965).

4

Significant contrasts and the teaching of pronunciation

We have previously mentioned the confusion between speech and writing, and we have taken the positive stand that the study of a spoken language cannot effectively be approached through writing. Rather, the spoken language must be considered *per se*, for language is primarily an oral-aural system of communication and sounds are the stuff of which it is made. The language teacher must therefore have a familiarity with, or better yet, a working knowledge of, sounds — how they are made by our organs of speech, how they are classified, and how they are used in the particular language of his interest. Many introductory textbooks in linguistics provide clear and logical explanations of the system used to describe sounds, which, although summarized in the following paragraphs, should eventually be more fully investigated by the serious student.[1]

If there were any assurance of scientific objectivity in it, a simple system for describing sounds could be evolved based on auditory impressions — the effect of each sound on the listener's ear. But what one

---

[1] Some sources are: Robert A. Hall, Jr., *Linguistics and Your Language* (New York: Doubleday Anchor Books A-201, 1960). Robert A. Hall, Jr., *Introductory Linguistics* (Philadelphia: Chilton, 1964), pp. 41–59. Robert Politzer and Charles Staubach, *Teaching Spanish: A Linguistic Orientation*, revised ed. (Boston: Blaisdell, 1965), chap. vi. David Abercrombie, *Elements of General Phonetics* (Chicago: Aldine, 1967).

person might describe as a "flat, harsh sound" may not be understood as such by another person, since terms such as "flat, broad, harsh" are too relative to have any objective reality. It would be like trying to describe chemical elements in terms of their smells.

As the use of sound spectrography becomes more widespread, linguists are growing better able to record and chart characteristics of sound waves as they occur in speech and to analyze more profitably the intensity, frequency, and other acoustic features of the sounds.[2] However, there is a highly effective system which can be used by the non-specialist as well as the specialist, based on the description of sounds, not according to their auditory impressions or acoustic characteristics, but in terms of the organs of the body used in producing them. Thus we may classify the sounds of a given language according to the speech organs involved and the ways in which they are used. This study is known as *articulatory phonetics*, since the analysis made is of the physiology of articulation.

To work with this system demands a knowledge of the organs of speech which are diagrammed below:

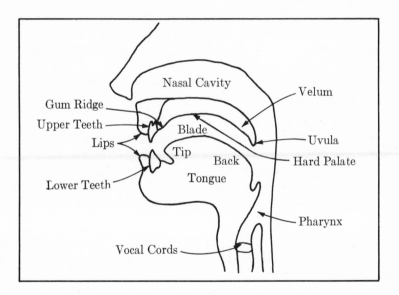

The organs of speech include essentially all the human respiratory tract. Air is drawn into and expelled from the lungs, which expand and con-

---

[2] Ernst Pulgram, *Introduction to the Spectrography of Speech* ('s Gravenhage: Mouton and Co., 1959).

tract under the influence of the diaphragm. As the breath moves to and from the lungs, it passes through the mouth, nasal cavity, pharynx, and trachea. These and other closely related parts of the body (such as the tongue and lips) are the organs customarily used in speech. The air passes in and out of the lungs in a stream or column, called the breath stream. The diagram above gives a cross-section of the human head and neck, showing the route that the breath stream follows on its way to and from the lungs, and the main organs of speech.

Within the area of the mouth, the organs of articulation are divided into two general categories: active articulators include those organs which actually move during the articulation of the sounds of the language: the tongue, the velum (also called the "soft palate"), and the lips. The velum is always active in that — since all Spanish sounds are either oral or nasal — it is raised or lowered in the production of nasal sounds. The velum is occasionally passive in that — after being raised or lowered — it then can form the passive surface against or toward which the dorsum of the tongue is raised. The passive articulators are those organs which do not move but with which the active articulators often come in contact: the palate and the teeth. By moving the active articulators, or by placing one or another of them in contact with specific passive articulators as the breath stream passes through them, all the sounds of a given language can be produced.

Among the sounds which the human organs of speech can generate there is a basic division:

a. Those sounds which can be made exclusively by forming resonance chambers in the mouth as a result of changing the position of the tongue. These are the sounds traditionally termed vowels.
b. Those sounds produced by obstructing the breath stream by the use of the active and passive organs of speech to produce audible friction. These are traditionally labelled consonants.

It is important to remember that here we are not speaking of the traditional orthographic vowels (a, e, i, o, u) and consonants (all the rest of the letters of the alphabet) but of vowel sounds and consonant sounds.

In making both types of sounds, we utilize variations in position of the organs of speech from the vocal cords upward. Three main factors are responsible for difference in sound:

a. The activity of the vocal cords.
b. The place or position in the mouth where a sound is articulated.
c. The manner in which it is articulated.

For every sound, we also distinguish three stages in its pronunciation: the *onset*, or time in which the organs of speech assume the position of its pronunciation; the *peak*, or time during which they are in that position; and the *coda*, or time in which they leave that position. In some languages some sounds differ only in the length of hold, or in the time of release.

After leaving the lungs, the breath stream passes between the vocal cords — two movable membranes which can either lie along the side of the larynx without making any sound (thus producing what are termed *voiceless* sounds, such as English and Spanish *p, t, f, s*), or may be brought together, either partially or completely, to set up sound waves and produce what are known as *voiced* sounds (usually all vowels and many consonants, like English and Spanish *b, d, m, l*).

Once it has passed the vocal cords on its way out of the lungs, the breath stream passes through various points in the pharynx, nose, and mouth where the column of air may be further modified.

In the nasal cavity there are no points at which an obstruction or other change in the breath stream can be made, but the whole nasal cavity can be brought into play as a resonance chamber (producing *nasalization*) or may be shut off from the course of the breath stream by the velum (whose movable tip is known as the *uvula*).

However, in the mouth (oral cavity) there are a number of ways the breath stream can be modified. The most active organ in these processes is undoubtedly the tongue, since it can be raised varying degrees at the front, middle, or back of its entire extension.

For vowel sounds the tongue does not come directly in contact with the roof of the mouth but assumes various positions inside the mouth to form cavities that serve as resonance chambers, conditioning the specific quality of the vowel sound. Two main factors determine the quality of the vowel: 1) whether it is the front, central or back part of the tongue which is raised, and 2) the height to which it is raised in the mouth. (Occasionally lip rounding and/or nasalization are also factors to be considered.)

Vowels, therefore, are usually classified by phoneticians according to two main features: tongue position (front, central, back) and tongue height (high, mid, low).

The tongue is also the principal organ in the pronunciation of consonants, but here other organs of speech (vocal cords, velum, uvula, hard palate, alveolar ridge, lips, and teeth) are also called into play. There are a number of special adjectives commonly applied to describe sounds articulated at the various points shown in the table on page 50.

TERM	REFERS TO	EXAMPLE (SPANISH)
uvular	uvula	*j* between back vowels (*ojo*)
velar	velum	*g* (*gato*); *c* (*cola*)
palatal	the area comprised of the alveolar ridge and the front portion of the hard palate	*ch, ñ*
alveolar	gum ridge	*s, n, r*
dental	teeth	*t, d*
labio-dental	lips and teeth	*f*
bilabial	lips	*p, m*

In addition to describing the *position* in which a sound is made, the linguist also distinguishes the *manner* in which it is articulated, since there are a number of ways in which the vocal cords, tongue, palate, etc., can obstruct the breath stream, either shutting it off completely or directing its passage through one kind of channel or another. The stream of breath may be *stopped* completely, as in English or Spanish ***p***, ***t***, ***k***; or it may be forced through a channel. This channel may take the form of a narrow *slit*, as in English ***f***, ***v***; or of a trough or depression (a *groove*) in the center of the tongue, as in English ***s***. The air may also pass over the depressed sides of the tongue, as in some kinds of ***l***. It may be modified by a single or repeated flap of some movable organ, like the lips (in the interjection usually written ***brrr***) or the tongue (in the Spanish *r*). Or the breath stream may be checked entirely in the oral cavity and while held the air escapes through the nasal cavity, using the nasal cavity as a resonance chamber, as in English ***m***, ***n***, and in the sound [ŋ] which we write with the letters ***ng*** (in *singing*).

Another set of adjectives, used to describe the various manners of articulation, is shown in the table on page 51.

While the stream of breath is being modified at a given point and in a given manner, as illustrated below, still other things may be happening at the same time. A puff of air may be sent out immediately after a consonant and produce a sound known as aspirated (like English ***p***, ***t***, ***k***). The sound may be directed into the nasal cavity for a fraction of a second before a consonant is articulated, coinciding with the onset of the sound, which is then termed a *prenasalized* consonant. This phenomenon may be observed in English by saying the word *and* very slowly and noting how the initial vowel /æ/ acquires the nasal quality as the articulatory organs prepare for the following /n/. If the tongue is raised close to the hard palate at the same time the consonant is articu-

TERM	REFERS TO SOUND PRONOUNCED WITH	EXAMPLE (SPANISH)
Stop or occlusive	Complete stoppage of breath stream	*b* /b/ (*bola*), *d* /d/ (*dar*) *p* /p/ (*pez*), *g* /g/ (*gota*) *c* /k/ (*hueco*)
Affricate	Release involving fricative (slit-type channel)	*ch* /č/ (*charla*)
Continuants made up of the following types:	No complete stoppage of breath stream	
Fricative	Slit-type channel Groove-type channel	*b* [ƀ] (*sabe*), g [ǥ] (*llegan*) *s* /s/ (*sala*)
Lateral	Channels over sides of tongue	*l* /l/ (*lana*)
Trill (vibrant)	One or more flaps of tongue	*r* /r/, *rr* /R/
Nasal	Nasal cavity as resonance chamber	*n* /n/, *m* /m/

lated, the consonant is said to be *palatalized*, as is the /d/ in the English word *education*.

Furthermore, sounds are pronounced with different degrees of intensity of air being expelled from the lungs. This feature, intensity, is termed stress and is of great significance since a change of stress may change the meaning of an utterance. Many English minimal pairs involve only a change in the position of stress, such as *prótest* vs. *protést*, etc.

Within the frame of reference elaborated thus far, the phonetician can describe and classify the sounds of any language. He might describe a sound as a "high tense front unrounded vowel" (which we usually write *i* in Spanish) or as "voiceless dental fricative" (which we normally spell *th* as in *thing* or what many Spaniards say for *z* in *caza*).

The phonetician found that this terminology, though it was the only scientific and universal way of describing a sound, was somewhat cumbersome. As chemistry had already shown, specific symbols could be assigned to represent elements, so the phoneticians devised a set of symbols, a one-to-one correspondence with each sound to be represented; this came to be known as a *phonetic transcription*. Each symbol was to stand for only one sound and each sound should be represented by only one symbol. Our traditional English and Spanish spelling systems or alphabets, based on the Roman alphabet, are inadequate to serve for phonetic transcription since the twenty-six letters could not begin to represent all the possible sounds. As a result, many systems of phonetic transcription were devised, such as Bell's "Visible Speech" and Pike's "Functional Analphabetic Symbolism" which abandoned all use of the Roman alphabet. However, most widely used phonetic transcriptions, such as the International Phonetic Alphabet (IPA), use the traditional Roman alphabet as a base and introduce new letters or alterations in the shape of familiar letters when the need arises. Those interested in phonetic symbols will find them readily available in a variety of books.[3]

The scientific reliability of the symbol in representing a sound and the ease with which the symbol may be used, made a phonetic transcription an essential tool for all work dealing with sounds. Between the years 1870 and 1920 phoneticians amassed a great body of knowledge for describing the pronunciation of sounds and for symbolizing them in transcription. Many beginning language textbooks included full phonetic transcription of the sounds of that language which the students were expected to master and to reproduce, sometimes to the confusion of the students, such as indeed was the case with one of the authors of this text who naïvely thought, in the first weeks of studying French as a youth, that he was actually writing French orthography when he was producing a phonetic transcription!

From 1920 on, however, after the research of men such as Edward Sapir and Leonard Bloomfield, linguists began to see that sounds are important only as they perform a specific function in the language by differentiating the meaning of words. Research was then concentrated on discovering and symbolizing not only speech sounds as such, but those functional units of speech sound that are significant, i.e., that make a difference in meaning. For such functional units of sound, the term *phoneme* was adopted.

In English, for instance, the words *bit* and *pit* each contain three significant units of sound, or phonemes, but differ from each other only in the first phoneme (cf. *beso* and *peso* in Spanish). Similarly, *bit* and *beat* each have three phonemes and differ only in the second phoneme (cf. Spanish *peso*, *paso*). By this method of contrasting pairs of words, specifically called *minimal pairs*, the linguist can establish a series of meaningful differences among words and each difference serves to set up a pair of contrasting phonemes.

For an individual sound functioning as part of a unit of sound, the term *allophone* (or *positional variant*) is used. As an example, let us take two sounds in many types of American English which are normally

---

[3] The best single source is *The Principles of the International Phonetic Association* (London: University College, 1949).

written as *l*, but are phonetically quite different: the alveolar variety found at the beginning of a syllable in words such as *lead* and *look* and the velar variety at the end of the syllable, in words like *wool* and *fool*. These sounds are represented by different phonetic symbols [l] and [ł], and the difference is easily discernible to anyone who is listening for it. But after studying the distribution patterns of these sounds within words, the linguist finds that [l] always occurs at the beginning of a syllable while [ł] is always found at the end of a syllable. Therefore these two sounds never make a difference in meaning between two words in English (cf. initial *d* in Spanish *dama*, which is a voiced stop, and intervocalic *d* in *nada*, which is a spirant). We therefore find the sounds represented by [l] and [ł] to be merely positional variants or allophones of the same phoneme. They are consequently not significant functional units of sound since they do not make a difference in meaning.

The stage of analysis described above is known as phonemics and has now been accepted by all linguists as an essential part of linguistic analysis. The symbolic representation of the phonemic analysis is known as *phonemic transcription* and the symbols are normally placed between slant lines: / / to distinguish them from phonetic transcription, which uses brackets: [ ], or from ordinary spelling.

Phonemics does not in any way supplant phonetics but simply builds further on the results obtained in phonetics with a change of emphasis. In essence, it is a simplification of the analysis of the sound system and represents a shift in aim — from that of representing every identifiable sound to that of representing only functionally significant units of sound. It has the advantage of not being cluttered up with non-essentials.

Since each language has its own organization, its own economy, the phonemes of one language are not the same as those of another. We find that the sounds of each language fall into a distinctive pattern and we cannot expect one language to have the same patterns as another. Any feature of sound may be highly significant in one language and completely without phonemic significance in another.

In general, more mature speakers of one language can hear and imitate without special training only those phonemic distinctions which their own language has taught them to be attentive to (the difference between *bad* and *bed*, important to the speaker of English, is scarcely perceptible to a Spaniard). In order to hear and make unfamiliar phonemic distinctions, we normally need to have our attention specially called to them and often have to be carefully instructed in the means of producing them.

With this in mind, the following chart of significant sounds of Spanish

SUMMARY OF THE SOUNDS OF AMERICAN SPANISH

MANNER	Bilabial (bilabial)		Labiodental (labiodental)		Dental (dental)		Alveolar (alveolar)		Palatal (palatal)		Velar (velar)	
	vl*	vd†	vl	vd	vl	vd	vl	vd	vl	vd	vl	vd
Stops (oclusivas)	/p/	/b/			/t/	/d/					/k/	/g/
Affricates (africadas)									/č/			
Fricatives (fricativas)		[β]	/f/			[đ]	/s/	[z]			/x/	[ǥ]
Nasals (nasales)		/m/				/n/				/ñ/		[ŋ]
Laterals (laterales)								/l/				
Trills (vibrantes)								/R/				
Flaps (vibrantes)								/r/				
Semiconsonants (semiconsonantes)		/w/								/y/		

POSITION

* vl, voiceless (sordo)
† vd, voiced (sonoro)

as spoken in the Western Hemisphere (the phonemes and allophones) has been prepared, utilizing the descriptive terms presented earlier in this chapter. The terms which appear in the vertical column at the left indicate the manner in which the sound is articulated. The terms in the horizontal row across the top of the diagram indicate the point at which the sound is articulated. Each vertical column is subdivided into *voiced* and *voiceless*. Thus we identify the sound /p/ as a *stop*, as a *bilabial*, since it is produced by stopping the flow of air from the lungs by bringing the lips together, and as *voiceless*, since the vocal cords are not vibrating as the sound is articulated.

With the aid of the information presented in this diagram the teacher will be able to utilize the principles of phonemics (significant contrasts) in the presentation and correction of pronunciation.

A system of charting, similar to the one we have used for the consonants, could be used for the vowels, with vertical categories referring to the relative height of the tongue (high, mid, or low), and horizontal categories referring to the appropriate area of the mouth (anterior, central, or posterior). To illustrate this, we may superimpose the diagram of the upper and lower jaws over the vowel chart:

SPANISH VOWEL PHONEMES

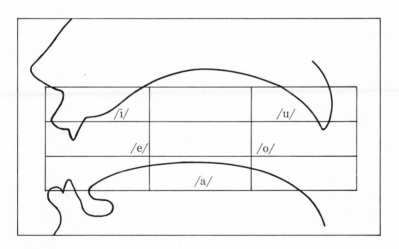

The following charts show the standard phonemic symbols for the vowel and consonant phonemes of Spanish and English and provide an example of each in the context of a word.

SPANISH PHONEMIC SYMBOLS		ENGLISH PHONEMIC SYMBOLS [4]	
Vowels		*Vowels*	
/i/	*sí*	/ɪ/	sit
/e/	*se*	/ɛ/	set
/a/	*sala*	/æ/	sat
/o/	*sol*	/a/	sot
/u/	*sur*	/ɔ/	sought
		/ʌ/	suck
		/U/	soot

English "long vowels," such as those in *say*, *see*, etc., are phonetically diphthongs: [eh], [iy], etc.

Consonants		*Consonants*	
/p/	*pato*	/p/	put
/t/	*todo*	/b/	buy
/k/	*codo*	/t/	took
/b/	*boda*	/d/	die
/d/	*dedo*	/k/	cook
/g/	*gota*	/g/	gain
/č/	*chula*	/č/	chill
/f/	*foto*	/ǰ/	gypsy
/s/	*salto*	/f/	foot
/x/	*jota*	/v/	vile
/m/	*mano*	/θ/	thing
/n/	*nada*	/ð/	though
/ñ/	*año*	/h/	who
/l/	*ala*	/s/	sing
/r/	*cara*	/z/	zone
/R/	*carro*	/š/	should
		/ž/	rouge
		/l/	long
		/m/	mat
		/n/	name
		/ŋ/	sing
		/r/	red
		/y/	young
		/w/	would

---

[4] For further discussion of the English vowel system, and especially of the treatment of the "long vowels," see Henry A. Gleason, Jr., *Introduction to Descriptive Linguistics*, revised ed. (Holt, Rinehart and Winston, 1961), chap. iii. The choice of

There are five simple (phonemic) vowels in Spanish. They are /i e a o u/, and we can demonstrate them to our classes in words such as *piso, peso, paso, poso*, and *puso*. English, on the other hand, may have from six to nine simple vowels and four to seven complex vowels, according to the dialect spoken. Many speakers of American English have seven simple and four complex vowels. However, none of the English vowels corresponds very closely to any of the five Spanish vowels. Traditionally, of course, a student seeing the written form *peso* might well have been expected to pronounce it using the nearest English equivalent, the result being a form like [peːzow]. Since we now have developed a teaching technique whereby the student does not meet the written representation of sounds until he already knows them, this kind of "spelling pronunciation" will be less frequent. The tendency still remains, however, for the English-speaking student to pronounce a Spanish vowel sound with the nearest English equivalent; or, in other words, to transfer his English habits into his Spanish pronunciation.

We have all heard our students pronounce [i] in Spanish *fin* either like the [ij] of English *meat*, or like the [ɪ] of English *mitt*. Neither one of the English vowels is an exact equivalent. Spanish /i/ falls somewhere between the two English vowels. In a similar way, the student will very likely replace the Spanish vowel /e/ with the English [ɛ] of *met* or with the [ej] of *bay*. The same kind of error will most likely be repeated with all stressed vowels.

Unstressed vowels and the consonants are subject to the same kind of transfer of habits.

The point is simply that there are no exact equivalents in the vowels and perhaps only two or three close approximations in the consonants of the two languages and that the student cannot rely directly upon English analogies. When our older textbooks begin a chapter on Spanish pronunciation by saying that the /i/ sound of Spanish *piso* is the same as the /iy/ sound of English *machine*, we know that, since the two sounds are not really alike, this is misleading the student and may well destroy the student's chances of acquiring a more nearly authentic ac-

---

symbols to represent the phonemes of a particular language is comparatively wide. Many systems have been developed and several of them are currently in use, according to the training and preference of the individual investigator. The interested reader may wish to consult Robert A. Hall, Jr., *Introductory Linguistics* (Philadelphia: Chilton, 1964), especially pp. 38–39 and 81, for a discussion of the principal systems now employed. The International Phonetic Alphabet, or some modification of it, is generally the basis for such systems. For an outline of the development of the IPA, the reader may wish to consult Robert W. Albright, *The International Phonetic Alphabet* (Bloomington: Indiana University Research Center in Anthropology, Folklore, and Linguistics, Publication #7, 1958).

cent. Of course, there are some points at which the careful use of English equivalents may be profitable. Much depends upon how and how much they are used. For example, some teachers find a convenient analogy between the sound represented by **dd** in *ladder* to help teach the correct point and manner of articulation of Spanish *r* in *toro*.

How, then, can the principles of significant contrasts help us to take a more realistic view of teaching pronunciation? First, we must know what muscular actions are involved in producing the sounds of Spanish. Although we do not need to have a physiologist's knowledge of speech organs, we must know the approximate position and shape of the lips and tongue, and whether the vocal cords are vibrating (for voiced sounds) or are not (for voiceless sounds). Second, we must have recourse to a competent analysis of the sounds of both English and Spanish to see which English sounds the English-speaking student will attempt to substitute for somewhat similar Spanish sounds.[5]

Once we have this information, we are ready to proceed to the technique itself. In general, the procedure is the same for teaching vowels and consonants: a pronunciation drill containing four steps, one of which, as we shall indicate, is optional, depending upon how well the students learn the sound from the beginning.[6]

1. Present the sound in a context, usually a word. Thus, if the sound to be taught is /i/, present it to the students in a list of forms, such as: *piso, liso, quiso, mito.* Of course, the students will repeat after the teacher's oral model (or a tape recording) and will not see the corresponding written symbols. The contextual presentation adheres to an important principle of the audio-lingual approach, which is to present forms in context — here, sounds in a context of actual

---

[5] Cf. J. D. Bowen and R. P. Stockwell, *Patterns of Spanish Pronunciation* (Chicago: University of Chicago Press, 1960), and the same authors' *The Sound Systems of English and Spanish* (Chicago: University of Chicago Press, 1964). For a more complete treatment of the sound system of Spanish, consult Tomás Navarro Tomás, *Manual de pronunciación española* (New York: Hafner Publishing Co., 1958). Some useful practice materials in Spanish pronunciation include the courses by Quilis, Rodríguez Castellano, and Badía Margarit.

[6] Whether or not these four steps are to be preceded by auditory discrimination exercises is a matter for the judgment of each individual teacher. The underlying idea is that learning to pronounce a foreign language is in essence learning to make differentiated responses to discriminative stimuli. Normally, this is accomplished by asking students to tell which of two closely related utterances they are hearing, e.g., *te lo dice* vs. *se lo dice.* The same technique can be applied to recognizing "acceptable" vs. "unacceptable" realizations of Spanish utterances. The effectiveness of auditory discrimination training is still under investigation. Cf. Paul Pimsleur, "Programming Acoustic Discriminatory Skills," in F. R. Morton, *Programming Audio-Lingual Skills* (Ann Arbor: University of Michigan, 1962).

Spanish words. Besides, the student is unconsciously practicing the pronunciation of the adjacent sounds. The method of repetition is as we have suggested before: teacher, students-in-chorus, teacher, students-in-chorus, teacher, individual student, teacher.

2. Present the sound in minimal contrast with another sound of the same class (vowel or consonant). Thus, if we continue with /i/, we shall ask the students to repeat pairs of utterances: *piso/peso; piso/paso; piso/puso*, etc. This enables the student not only to hear the difference, but also to feel the changed position of the articulatory organs. The method of repetition is as suggested above.

3. Present the sound in a more complex context. Continuing with /i/, hide it in a larger phrase, such as *él no vino*. This helps us to make sure that the student has really mastered the sound and that, when he is forced to articulate a longer chain of sounds, his correct response is really automatic.

4. Because of the tendency to transfer English speech habits into Spanish, which we have already discussed, a few students will still substitute a near-English sound for the Spanish sound, even after the above three steps are completed. Such students need an exercise in contrasting the English sound with the desired Spanish one. Such a contrastive exercise generally suffices to make the student aware of the physical difference (the difference in the organs and muscles he uses) that causes the difference in sound which his ear had failed to detect before (during the earlier exercises). This exercise again uses minimal pairs, but, now, one member of the pair is Spanish and the other, English: **sin**/*sin*, **son**/*son*, **que**/*Kay*, etc. If necessary, the teacher can explain which speech organs are involved and how they are placed.

With the consonants, the problems may be different, but the same four-step technique we have been discussing gives good results. Here, we may also use visual devices and demonstrations to reinforce practice. For example, we know that English /p/ is aspirated, but Spanish /p/ is not. We can explain to the student that "aspirated" means an articulation followed by a breath of air, but some students find the concept easier to grasp when the teacher holds a piece of onionskin paper in front of his mouth (with the paper touching the tip of his nose) and says the English word *papa*. The paper will flutter when the first /p/ is sounded. (Depending on the individual, the second /p/ may also be sufficiently aspirated to cause the paper to move again.) The Spanish word *papá*, with unaspirated /p/'s, will not cause the paper to move. Many teachers have devised ingenious methods of demonstrating these phonetic concepts and any such visual aid is helpful, provided that it is based on sound phonological principles.

To build a small file of dependable phonological exercises, a small project is suggested using a packet or two of 4 x 6 cards. For each of the phonological contrasts on the next pages, the teacher should make a set of ten minimal pairs on one card. The heading on each card, upper right, should indicate the contrast being illustrated, according to the following diagram. The cards can then be filed and used in class for an introductory pronunciation drill, or to redrill the class whenever pronunciation errors recur.

/u/	vs.	/a/
puso		paso
puñal		pañal
pulidez		palidez
cura		cara

Outline of Principal Significant Contrasts for Drill

I. **Vowel contrasts.**
   A. Stressed. (An accent mark in these lists refers to a stressed vowel and does not necessarily correspond to the orthographic accent.)

   1. In isolation.   (example)
      | /í/ | piso |
      | /é/ | peso |
      | /á/ | paso |
      | /ó/ | pozo |
      | /ú/ | puso |

   2. Contrasted with one another.
      | /í/ vs. /é/ | piso vs. peso |
      | /í/ vs. /ó/ | piso vs. pozo |
      | /í/ vs. /á/ | piso vs. paso |
      | /í/ vs. /ú/ | piso vs. puso |
      | /é/ vs. /á/ | peso vs. paso |
      | /é/ vs. /ó/ | peso vs. pozo |
      | /é/ vs. /ú/ | peso vs. puso |
      | /á/ vs. /ó/ | paso vs. pozo |
      | /á/ vs. /ú/ | paso vs. puso |
      | /ó/ vs. /ú/ | pozo vs. puso |

B. Unstressed. (In actual drill, we must be extremely careful not
to let the natural tendency to highlight the vowel in question
cause us to stress it. It is wise to warn the students about this
as well.)

1. In isolation. (example)

/i/	pisó
/e/	pesó
/a/	pasó
/o/	posó
/u/	puzól

2. Contrasted with one another.

/i/ *vs.* /e/	ligar *vs.* legar
/i/ *vs.* /o/	mirar *vs.* morar
/i/ *vs.* /a/	ligar *vs.* lagar
/i/ *vs.* /u/	ligar *vs.* lugar
/e/ *vs.* /a/	legar *vs.* lagar
/e/ *vs.* /o/	pesar *vs.* posar
/e/ *vs.* /u/	legar *vs.* lugar
/a/ *vs.* /o/	pasé *vs.* posé
/a/ *vs.* /u/	lagar *vs.* lugar
/o/ *vs.* /u/	morar *vs.* murar

C. Diphthongs.

/é/ *vs.* /éj/	le *vs.* ley
/á/ *vs.* /áj/	bala *vs.* baila
/ó/ *vs.* /ój/	o *vs.* hoy
/á/ *vs.* /áw/	ala *vs.* aula
/é/ *vs.* /éw/	dedo *vs.* deudo

D. English interference.

1. English diphthong   Spanish vowel

/ej/	/e/	(lay *for* le)
/ow/	/o/	(low *for* lo)
/ij/	/i/	(seen *for* sin)
/uw/	/u/	(too *for* tu)

2. English diphthong   Spanish diphthong

/ɛy/	/ej/	(lay *for* ley)
/ɑy/	/aj/	(eye *for* hay)
/ɔy/	/oj/	(boy *for* voy)
/ɑw/	/aw/	(owl *for* aula)

3. English vowel   Spanish vowel

/æ/	/a/	(plan *for* plan)
/ɔ/	/o/	(call *for* col)
/ɪ/	/i/	(Italy *for* Italia)

II. Consonant contrasts.

A. Little apparent difficulty, therefore minimum drill.

/m/	/f/	[z]	/b/	/g/
me	fé	mismo	¡Basta!	¡Gol!

B. The following consonants are articulated at approximately the same points in English and Spanish. The problem is that the English consonants are aspirated and the Spanish are not. Therefore, contrastive drill is indicated.

English consonant *vs.* Spanish consonant[7]

/p/	/p/	(pan *vs.* pan)
/k/	/k/	(cone *vs.* con)

C. In the following consonants the manner of articulation is the same as in English, but the place is slightly different.

	English	Spanish
/n/	alveolar	dental
/d/	alveolar	dental
/č/	palatal	alveolo-palatal
/y/	lenis palatal	fortis alveolo-palatal
	(lenis: with lesser raising of the laminum)	(fortis: with greater raising of the laminum)
/ñ/	lenis palatal nasal	fortis alveolo-palatal nasal

D. In the pronunciation of the following consonants, both the place and manner of articulation change from Spanish to English.

	English	Spanish
/t/	alveolar aspirated	dental non-aspirated
/r/	post-alveolar with dorsal groove	alveolar flap
/l/	alveolar	dental

---

[7] English /p/ and /k/ in other than initial position are not aspirated and are therefore closer to their Spanish counterparts.

E. The following Spanish consonants are best taught in isolation.

/b/	cabo
/g/	vago
/d/	cada
/R/	carro
/x/	faja

Additional material to complete the sets may be found in Bowen and Stockwell, *Patterns of Spanish Pronunciation* (see Bibliography), in *Modern Spanish*, and in the Teacher's Manual accompanying the *A-LM* texts.

▶ EXERCISES

1. Discuss the principal pedagogical value of describing the sounds of a language in terms of their point and manner of articulation.
2. Discuss why the sounds of Spanish cannot be taught effectively by relating each sound to an equivalent, or nearly equivalent, sound in English, e.g. Spanish /a/ in *pato* with English /a/ in *father*.
3. Discuss the relative importance of the respiratory, oral, and nasal organs in the articulation of the sounds of Spanish.
4. Discuss the importance of the principle of "significant contrasts."
5. Pinpoint the ways in which the English vocalic system interferes in learning directly the pronunciation of Spanish vowels.
6. Make a list of nineteen Spanish consonants and describe the articulatory features that pertain to each one. For example:

/p/   voiceless bilabial stop

7. The tendency to transfer the English phonemic system into Spanish causes problems we can anticipate. Name at least five such specific problems and indicate by what techniques we may resolve them.
8. Should a phonemic transcription of the target language be avoided in the beginning text since it might be more confusing to the language learner than a phonetic transcription or traditional orthography would be? Which alternate solutions exist?

REFERENCE BOOKS AND ARTICLES

ALARCOS LLORACH, EMILIO. *Fonología española* (Madrid: Gredos, 1954).

BEYM, RICHARD. "Practical Phonetic Orientation for Effective Spoken Spanish" (*Hispania* XLIII, 1960), 67–69.

BOLINGER, DWIGHT L. "English Prosodic Stress and Spanish Sentence Order" (*Hispania* XXXVII, 1954), 152–156.

BOWEN, J. DONALD and ROBERT P. STOCKWELL. *Patterns of Spanish Pronunciation* (Chicago: University of Chicago Press, 1960).

―――. *The Sounds of English and Spanish* (Chicago: University of Chicago Press, 1964).

CÁRDENAS, DANIEL N. *Introducción a una comparación fonológica del español y del inglés* (Washington, D.C.: Center for Applied Linguistics, 1960).

DE ENTRAMBASAGUAS, JOAQUÍN. *Síntesis de pronunciación española* (Madrid: CSIC, 1952).

HADEN, ERNEST F. *How to Pronounce Spanish* (New York: Holt, 1953).

LADO, ROBERT. "A Comparison of the Sound Systems of English and Spanish" (*Hispania* XXXIX, 1956), 26–29.

LÉON, PIERRE. "Teaching Pronunciation," in Albert Valdman, ed., *Trends in Language Teaching* (New York: McGraw-Hill, 1965).

NAVARRO, TOMÁS. *Manual de pronunciación española* (New York: Hafner, 1958).

―――. *Manual de entonación española* (New York: Hispanic Institute, 1948).

POLITZER, ROBERT L. and CHARLES N. STAUBACH. *Teaching Spanish: A Linguistic Orientation*, revised ed. (Waltham, Mass.: Blaisdell, 1965), especially chap. vi.

5

$\mathcal{S}$yntactic drills

The fundamental skills approach to the teaching of syntax centers about two features: carefully constructed dialogues into which the syntactic patterns are woven and which the students are expected to memorize, and drills of rather definite types which embody the patterns and make them habitual by varying them in systematic ways. Of course, even with the more traditional textbook, these same kinds of drills still give excellent results; so it is well for the individual teacher to know how to make and use them, regardless of the textbook being used.

The structural focuses of any given unit in the audio-lingual text are determined by the structure embodied in the dialogue of the same unit. The point of departure for each syntactic (or pattern or structure) drill is always the basic dialogue in which the structure occurred. In this way, the drill becomes an inductive learning experience in which the student, after having practiced, memorized, and habituated the basic sentence in which a particular syntactic structure has appeared in natural, native context, learns how to manipulate the same structure in different analogous situations. Note that we do not attempt to generalize a "rule"; rather we allow the pattern to emerge by conditioned variation within an understandable context.

The reader may wish to review Section VI of the Sample Skeleton Audio-Lingual Unit presented in Chapter 2, in which we deal with drills. The grammatical point being presented in any given drill is manipulated in such a way that the items which comprise the drill are varied without changing the essential structure of the original model utterance. Therefore, the student's attention is focused on the slot where the changes are to be made; he learns to handle the item that can be substituted in the slot and gradually develops an understanding of the pattern being drilled.

Let us now examine the fundamental method by which syntactic drills of the type we are discussing are built. First, the audio-lingual structure drill begins with a model utterance or "frame" which the class always repeats in chorus after the teacher's model, at the beginning of the exercise. For example, the frame **el niño corre** can form a point of departure for the verb-form exercise:

Teacher (model)	**El niño corre.**
Class (echo)	**El niño corre.**
Teacher (cue)	**Los niños** _____
Class (response)	**Los niños corren.**
Teacher (cue)	**Yo** _____
Class (response)	**Yo corro.**

In reverse, the same frame serves as a point of departure for the singular and plural subject exercise:

Teacher (model)	**El niño corre.**
Class (echo)	**El niño corre.**
Teacher (cue)	_____ **corren.**
Class (response)	**Los niños corren.**
Teacher (cue)	_____ **corro.**
Class (response)	**Yo corro.**

Obviously in the syntactical points illustrated above, there is no difference between this structure in English and in Spanish. The student quickly grasps the syntactical point since the structure in English would produce an identical frame: "The children run." The difference is only in the words that occupy the positions in the frame. At the other extreme are utterances like "I like to read" and **me gusta leer.** Here the frames are in contrast. Naturally the drills used to demonstrate points of similarity will be short (remember how the same criterion was applied to the "significant contrasts" of the sound system), and those drills which teach more complex differences will be longer, to avoid foreign-sounding phrases or perhaps even a breakdown in communication.

We now turn to the various types of drills and frames. We shall begin with a simple frame, here called Frame A, composed of a subject and predicate of one word each: **Juan habla.** Let us suppose that the utterance was presented in the basic dialogue (our first rule for the composition of drills); also present in the dialogue might be such words as **María, Eduardo, Celia,** and the verb forms **escribe, come,** and **lee.** The name "slot" is given to the position occupied by each word in the basic frame. Frame A therefore has two slots. If one slot is held constant, and a substitution is made in the other slot, using forms presented in the dialogue, we may construct drills such as:

Teacher (model)	**Juan habla.**
Class (Echo)	**Juan habla.**
Teacher (cue)	**María** _____
Class (response)	**María habla.**
Teacher (cue)	**Eduardo** _____
Class (response)	**Eduardo habla**
	etc.

Or we may maintain constant the first slot and substitute the verb form in the second:

Teacher (model)	**Juan habla.**
Class (echo)	**Juan habla.**
Teacher (cue)	_____ **escribe.**
Class (response)	**Juan escribe.**
Teacher (cue)	_____ **lee.**
Class (response)	**Juan lee.**
Teacher (cue)	_____ **come.**
Class (response)	**Juan come.**

We can easily see how more than one word could fill the other slot without changing the frame in any way. If we extend our search, we may find that words other than the names of people can occupy the initial position in Frame A, such as **mi amigo, el niño, el profesor.**

The drills presented above are examples of the *simple substitution drill.* The simple substitution in one or another slot in a given frame offers a wide variety of drills in which the syntactic structure of the frame is not changed. Below are further illustrations:[1]

1. Substitution of noun, drilling use of definite article:

Teacher (model)	**Estamos con el cónsul.**
Class (echo)	**Estamos con el cónsul.**

---

[1] Bolinger *et al., op. cit.,* p. 26 and p. 23.

Teacher (cue)	_____ hermano.
Class (response)	**Estamos con el hermano.**
Teacher (cue)	_____ papá.
Class (response)	**Estamos con el papá.**
Teacher (cue)	_____ tía.
Class (response)	**Estamos con la tía.**
Teacher (cue)	_____ mamá.
Class (response)	**Estamos con la mamá.**, etc.

2. Substitution involving person and number of verbs:

Teacher (model)	**Yo no hablo inglés.**
Class (echo)	**Yo no hablo inglés.**
Teacher (cue)	**Nosotros** _____
Class (response)	**Nosotros no hablamos inglés.**
Teacher (cue)	**Él** _____
Class (response)	**Él no habla inglés.**
Teacher (cue)	**Ellas** _____
Class (response)	**Ellas no hablan inglés.**
	etc.

The frame from 2 above could also be used to drill vocabulary, by holding the first slot constant and varying the object slot (in the example below, the names of languages):

Teacher (model)	**Yo no hablo inglés.**
Class (echo)	**Yo no hablo inglés.**
Teacher (cue)	_____ alemán.
Class (response)	**Yo no hablo alemán.**
Teacher (cue)	_____ francés.
Class (response)	**Yo no hablo francés.**
	etc.

The simple substitution drill may be elaborated into a progressive substitution drill, where the same frame is used, but the constant slot and the variation slot are alternated, such as the following drill found on page 27 of *Modern Spanish*, second edition:[2]

Teacher (model)	**La chica está en la sala.**
Class (echo)	**La chica está en la sala.**
Teacher (cue)	_____ chico _____
Class (response)	**El chico está en la sala.**

---

[2] *Ibid.*

Teacher (cue)	_____ **cuarto.**
Class (response)	**El chico está en el cuarto.**
Teacher (cue)	_____ **chica** _____
Class (response)	**La chica está en el cuarto.**
Teacher (cue)	_____ **patio.**
Class (response)	**La chica está en el patio.**
Teacher (cue)	_____ **cocina.**
Class (response)	**La chica está en la cocina.**
	etc.

The purpose of the foregoing exercise is to drill the student in the use of the masculine and feminine definite articles. But the same type of progressive substitution drill can easily be adapted to, let us say, a verb and object exercise, alternating the variation slot:

Teacher (model)	**Yo no hablo inglés.**
Class (echo)	**Yo no hablo inglés.**
Teacher (cue)	**Tú** _____
Class (response)	**Tú no hablas inglés.**
Teacher (cue)	_____ **francés.**
Class (response)	**Tú no hablas francés.**
Teacher (cue)	**Él** _____
Class (response)	**Él no habla francés.**
	etc.

Frames need not be limited to two slots only. The frame **Juan habla español** by simple substitution gives us three possible variants, i.e., holding two slots constant and varying one. Thus, with the first slot varied:

> **Juan** habla español.
> **María** habla español.
> **Celia** habla español.

With the second slot varied:

> Juan **habla** español.
> Juan **estudia** español.
> Juan **es** español.

With the third slot varied:

> Juan habla **español.**
> Juan habla **alemán.**
> Juan habla **chino.**

The same frame for progressive substitution gives us the ability to alternate the two constant slots and one varied slot:

Juan es **español.**
Juan es francés.
Carlos **es** francés.
Carlos habla **francés.**

Using the same frame as in the above drill, an elaborate progressive substitution drill (sometimes called a "combined pattern replacement drill") can be made dealing with vocabulary, person and number of verbs, and gender of adjectives:

Teacher (model)	**Juan es español.**
Class (echo)	**Juan es español.**
Teacher (cue)	**_____ habla _____**
Class (response)	**Juan habla español.**
Teacher (cue)	**Yo _____**
Class (response)	**Yo hablo español.**
Teacher (cue)	**_____ estudio _____**
Class (response)	**Yo estudio español.**
Teacher (cue)	**Mis amigos _____**
Class (response)	**Mis amigos estudian español.**
Teacher (cue)	**_____ alemán.**
Class (response)	**Mis amigos estudian alemán.**
Teacher (cue)	**Mi _____**
Class (response)	**Mi amigo estudia alemán.**
Teacher (cue)	**_____ es _____**
Class (response)	**Mi amigo es alemán.**
Teacher (cue)	**_____ alemanes.**
Class (response)	**Mis amigos son alemanes.**
Teacher (cue)	**Pablo _____**
Class (response)	**Pablo es alemán.**
Teacher (cue)	**María _____**
Class (response)	**María es alemana.**

In progressive substitution drills, care must be taken not to provide a cue that can fit more than one slot. For example, in a frame such as **María ve a Susana, Celia** could fit either the subject or the object slot, making two responses possible. Progressive substitution drills are especially valuable at the end of a given unit of study, as a review or test.

The last two examples given above are substitution drills, but they are also what are known as *correlation drills*. A correlation drill involves aligning the words that go into the slots so as to make them "agree." A word of explanation is in order here to show how correlation drills differ from simple substitution drills. In **Juan habla,** we have a normal frame, which might equally well be represented by **María habla** or by **Pablo canta.** This is because the category of words represented by **Juan** (**María, el hombre,** etc.) can "co-occur" with the category of words represented by **habla** (**canta, trabaja,** etc.) — which is simply to say that nouns can co-occur with verbs. This kind of co-occurrence of compatibility within a frame is called "constructional co-occurrence." Sometimes, individual words will not match up with other individual words — for example, while we might say **El dinero habla,** we would not normally say **El acero habla** (we use the asterisk to indicate that the utterance so marked is not a normal Spanish sequence); but this is a matter of individual co-occurrence, not of constructional co-occurrence. Within each of the categories, however, there are formal changes that must also be controlled to make them match — we can say **El hombre habla,** but not **Los hombres habla,** in spite of the fact that **hombres** is a noun and **habla** is a verb, and nouns can occur with verbs. Here, what has gone wrong is what has been termed a matter of "flexional co-occurrence": singular calls for singular, and plural for plural. Here is an example of a simple correlation drill with the lexical item in position 2 correlated with position 1:

Teacher	**Federico lee.**
Students	**Federico lee.**
Teacher	**Los niños** _____
Students	**Los niños leen.**

This parallels the technique of the simple substitution drill. There our parallel ends, however, since in the case of the simple correlation drill dealing with agreement, the word in position 1 (in this case the subject of the verb) determines or "governs" the word in position 2 (the verb), but not vice versa. In other words, a simple correlation drill involves changing the "governing" rather than the "governed" word. Replacement of the governed words leads us back to the simple substitution drill. The correlation drill, as we have seen, has the effect of conjugating verbs. And the more forms a tense has, the more valuable the simple correlation drill is. It provides more adequately than any traditional drills for practice in correlating person, gender, and number between verb-forms and subjects. In the first correlation drill above, we correlated the lexical item in position 2 with that in position 1. In the following drill, a *progressive correlation drill*, lexical items in position 1 are progressively correlated with lexical items in position 2.

Teacher	**Antonia saluda.**
Students	**Antonia saluda.**
Teacher	**_____ habla.**
Students	**Antonia habla.**
Teacher	**Jesús _____**
Students	**Jesús habla.**
Teacher	**_____ lee.**
Students	**Jesús lee.**
Teacher	**Carlos y Consuelo _____**
Students	**Carlos y Consuelo leen.**

When we want to have students practice the conjugation of one tense of one verb, we use the simple correlation drill. When we want to give them practice in one or more tenses of one or more verbs, we use the progressive correlation drill. We are in no way limited to one tense, either. A progressive correlation drill may be constructed to give a synopsis of one verb in several tenses. First, we may correlate lexical items in position 1 with items in position 2:

Teacher	**Adolfo canta.**
Students	**Adolfo canta.**
Teacher	**_____ cantó.**
Students	**Adolfo cantó.**
Teacher	**Ángel _____**
Students	**Ángel cantó.**
Teacher	**_____ cantará.**
Students	**Ángel cantará.**
Teacher	**Pedro y Carlos _____**
Students	**Pedro y Carlos cantarán.**

Second, we may correlate items in position 2 with those in position 1, thus drilling several verbs, varying both in number and in tense:

Teacher (model)	**Pablo lee el libro.**
Class (echo)	**Pablo lee el libro.**
Teacher (cue)	**_____ leyó _____**
Class (response)	**Pablo leyó el libro.**

Teacher (cue)	**Nosotros** _____
Class (response)	**Nosotros leímos el libro.**
Teacher (cue)	_____ **compramos** _____
Class (response)	**Nosotros compramos el libro.**
Teacher (cue)	**Pedro y Luisa** _____
Class (response)	**Pedro y Luisa compraron el libro.**
Teacher (cue)	_____ **compraré** _____
Class (response)	**Yo compraré el libro.**

This last example raises the question of what kind of item can be substituted in a slot. As you can see, the single word **Pablo** has been replaced by **nosotros** and later by the conjunctive phrase **Pedro y Luisa**. This does not violate any principle of drill construction, since the slots themselves remain intact and the frame is unaffected.

We should now call attention to four variations which may occur within a given structural slot:

1. A replacement involves the substitution of one or more words which differ completely in form from the original entry. Thus we say we "replace" **Juan** by **Alberto, el hombre,** or **él;** or **habla** by **llora, lee,** or **canta,** in Frames A and B below:

A.	Teacher (model)	**Juan habla**
	Class (echo)	**Juan habla**
	Teacher (cue)	**Alberto** _____
	Class (response)	**Alberto habla.**
	Teacher (cue)	**El hombre** _____
	Class (response)	**El hombre habla.**
	Teacher (cue)	**Él** _____
	Class (response)	**Él habla.**
B.	Teacher (model)	**Juan habla.**
	Class (echo)	**Juan habla.**
	Teacher (cue)	_____ **llora.**
	Class (response)	**Juan llora.**
	Teacher (cue)	_____ **lee.**
	Class (response)	**Juan lee.**
	Teacher (cue)	_____ **canta.**
	Class (response)	**Juan canta.**

2. An expansion involves adding modifiers to, or otherwise extending the length of, the slot. Thus, **los consejos, los buenos consejos,**

and **sus muy buenos consejos** are possible expansions of the word **consejos** in the frame **Nos dió consejos.** Each of the three slots filled by a single word in the frame **Roberto habla francés** may be expanded to include two or more words, as happens with the subject slot in the following example:

Teacher (model)	**Roberto habla francés.**
Students (echo)	**Roberto habla francés.**
Teacher (cue)	**Él** _____
Students (response)	**Él habla francés.**
Teacher (cue)	**El hombre** _____
Students (response)	**El hombre habla francés.**
Teacher (cue)	**El dueño** _____
Students (response)	**El dueño habla francés.**
Teacher (cue)	**El dueño simpático** _____
Students (response)	**El dueño simpático habla francés.**
Teacher (cue)	**El dueño simpático de la tienda** _____
Students (response)	**El dueño simpático de la tienda habla francés.**
Teacher (cue)	**El dueño simpático de la tienda que fuma un cigarrillo** _____
Students (response)	**El dueño simpático de la tienda que fuma un cigarrillo habla francés.**

The expanded subject in the last response of the above drill is the same basic syntactical structure (the subject of the utterance) whose drill was begun by the simple frame **Roberto habla francés.** In the example below, slots 1, 2, and 3 are progressively replaced and expanded:

Teacher (model)	**Roberto habla francés.**
Class (echo)	**Roberto habla francés.**
Teacher (cue)	**Él** _____
Class (response)	**Él habla francés.**
Teacher (cue)	_____ **aprendió** _____
Class (response)	**Él aprendió francés.**
Teacher (cue)	_____ **idiomas.**
Class (response)	**Él aprendió idiomas.**
Teacher (cue)	_____ **estudió** _____
Class (response)	**Él estudió idiomas.**
Teacher (cue)	**El hombre** _____
Class (response)	**El hombre estudió idiomas.**

Teacher (cue)	_____ varios _____
Class (response)	**El hombre estudió varios idiomas.**
Teacher (cue)	_____ sabio _____
Class (response)	**El hombre sabio estudió varios idiomas.**
Teacher (cue)	_____ estudiará _____
Class (response)	**El hombre sabio estudiará varios idiomas.**
Teacher (cue)	_____ difíciles.
Class (response)	**El hombre sabio estudiará varios idiomas difíciles.**

The last steps of this drill involve the expansion of the complement from **idiomas** to **varios idiomas** and finally to **varios idiomas difíciles.**

3. In reduction, the same type of drill as the one given above could be done in reverse by starting with the last sentence and progressively reducing by replacement until we have returned to the basic frame.

4. An alteration is a change in the ending of the original entry: e.g., **lloró** for **llora** in the frame **Adolfo llora.**

It is important to realize that any drill may utilize a combination of these structures without violating the syntactical pattern established in the basic frame (the lengthy drill above was a substitution drill involving both replacement and expansion). Below we observe another example of a simple substitution drill involving replacement and expansion:

Teacher (model)	**Eliseo habla turco.**
Students (echo)	**Eliseo habla turco.**
Teacher (cue)	**Él _____**
Students (response)	**Él habla turco.**
Teacher (cue)	**El hombre _____**
Students (response)	**El hombre habla turco.**
Teacher (cue)	**El alcalde _____**
Students (response)	**El alcalde habla turco.**
Teacher (cue)	**El buen alcalde _____**
Students (response)	**El buen alcalde habla turco.**
Teacher (cue)	**El buen alcalde de nuestra ciudad _____**
Students (response)	**El buen alcalde de nuestra ciudad habla turco.**

Here is an example of a three-part progressive substitution drill involving replacement and expansion:

Teacher (model)	**Eliseo habla turco.**
Class (echo)	**Eliseo habla turco.**

Teacher (cue)	**Él** _____
Class (response)	**Él habla turco.**
Teacher (cue)	_____ **aprendió** _____
Class (response)	**Él aprendió turco.**
Teacher (cue)	_____ **muchas lenguas.**
Class (response	**Él aprendió muchas lenguas.**
Teacher (cue)	**El nuevo director** _____
Class (response)	**El nuevo director aprendió muchas lenguas.**

The processes of replacement, expansion, reduction and alteration are combined in both simple and progressive drills to meet the needs of specific drill focuses.

Until now we have been considering various kinds of cued drill procedures designed to produce a regularly alternating single structural change in some frame used as a base. Substitution and correlation drills were best suited for these purposes. Now we shall present several drill procedures which use a different sentence as a base for every step in the drill. These drills fall into three general catagories: transformation drills, question-answer drills, and translation drills. The term "transformation" is used here as a name of a specific drill and should not be confused with "transformation grammar."

1. *Transformation drills.* Below are a few of the many possible transformation drills:

   A. A verb in the present indicative tense transformed into simple past tense. In the following drill it will be observed that the verbs in the present tense have been deliberately selected to provide a variety of past tense forms, including irregular verbs. This type of advanced exercise assumes that each type of regular and irregular verb has been practiced separately in substitution, correlation, and transformation drills before the following drill is introduced:

Teacher's cue	Students' transformation
Luisa mira a su papá.	**Luisa miró a su papá.**
Roberto se acuesta temprano.	**Roberto se acostó temprano.**
Mis amigos me escriben.	**Mis amigos me escribieron.**
Voy a la fiesta.	**Fui a la fiesta.**

B. Possessive adjective transformed to the long form as predicate adjective:

Teacher's cue	Students' transformation
Éste es mi coche.	**Este coche es mío.**
Éstas son tus blusas.	**Estas blusas son tuyas.**
Señora, éste es su cuarto.	**Señora, este cuarto es suyo.**
Ésta es nuestra casa.	**Esta casa es nuestra.**

C. Word substitution transformations of direct or indirect object pronouns:

Teacher's cue	Students' transformation
Llamamos **a María.**	**La** llamamos.
Doy **el libro** a Pablo.	**Lo** doy a Pablo.
Doy **el libro a Pablo.**	**Se lo** doy.

2. **Question-answer drills.** These drills are divided into two categories: those containing questions which elicit the response *yes* or *no*, and those eliciting a response other than *yes* or *no*.

A. Questions eliciting *yes* or *no*:

Instructor asks	Student responds
¿Quiere Vd. ir a la fiesta?	**Sí, quiero ir.**
	Sí, quiero ir a la fiesta.
	No, no quiero.
¿Has visto a María?	**Sí, la he visto.**
	Sí, la vi ayer.
¿Le gustan las tortillas?	**Sí, me gustan mucho.**
	No, no me gustan las tortillas.

B. The question-answer drills which elicit a response other than *yes* or *no* are further divided into three groups:

(1) Information questions, free response:

Instructor asks	Student responds
¿Adónde fueron Vds. anoche?	**Fuimos al teatro,** etc.
¿Cuándo llegarán tus abuelos?	**Llegarán el sábado.**
	Van a llegar mañana.
¿Por qué no vino Alberto a la clase?	**Estaba enfermo.**
	Debe de estar en casa.

(2) Controlled-response questions:

Instructor asks	Student responds
¿Prefiere Vd. pan o tortillas?	**Prefiero pan.**
¿Quiere Vd. que me marche o que me quede?	**Quiero que se marche.**
¿Compraste los guantes o la cartera?	**Compré la cartera.**

The student may either respond with a free choice of one or the other, or may be cued by the use of hand signals to indicate that he should answer with the first or the second choice.

(3) Cued-response questions:

Instructor asks	Student responds
(la revista) ¿Qué quieres leer?	**Quiero leer la revista.**
(el cine) ¿Adónde van Vds. esta noche?	**Vamos al cine.**
(mis hermanos) ¿Quiénes llegaron ayer?	**Llegaron mis hermanos.**

3. **Translation drills.** These drills may be of several types. Extreme caution must be used in deciding those few cases in which translation drills are useful. Their over-use is contrary to the audio-lingual approach.

A. They may be used to point out differences in structure between the source and target languages, such as:

Instructor says	Student responds
Me gusta bailar.	**Me gusta bailar.**
I like to eat.	**Me gusta comer.**
We like to talk.	**Nos gusta hablar.**
He likes to read.	**Le gusta leer.**
He likes soup.	**Le gusta la sopa.**
We like the apartment.	**Nos gusta el apartamento.**
We like the suits.	**Nos gustan los trajes.**
I like the suits.	**Me gustan los trajes.**
I like to dance.	**Me gusta bailar.**

B. Translation drills are only one of the ways to approach the problem of teaching structures in which changes of word order in Spanish convey meanings which in English are accomplished by changing intonation:

Instructor says [3]	Student responds
There goes the new *maid*.	**Allá va la nueva criada.**
There goes the *new* maid.	**Allá va la criada nueva.**
There goes the *brand-new* car.	**Allá va el coche nuevo.**
It's his only suit.	**Es su único traje.**
It's his one and only suit.	**Es su traje único.**
It's pure air (*nothing but air*).	**Es puro aire.**
It's pure air (*uncontaminated*).	**Es aire puro.**
What are they drinking, just milk?	**¿Qué toman? ¿Pura leche?**
What are they drinking, pure milk?	**¿Qué toman? ¿Leche pura?**

C. The following drill summarizes some uses of the subjunctive in noun clauses where English uses an infinitive construction:

Instructor says	Student responds
Le pedí a mi hermana que cantara.	**Le pedí a mi hermana que cantara.**
I asked my brother to leave.	**Le pedí a mi hermano que saliera.**
I asked my mother to call me.	**Le pedí a mi madre que me llamara.**
I asked the professor to give me the book.	**Le pedí al profesor que me diera el libro.**
I asked my friends not to come to my house.	**Les pedí a mis amigos que no vinieran a mi casa.**

Four additional pattern drill types (essentially variations of the major types we have been discussing) appear frequently in audio-lingual texts and are used for specific types of learning objectives:

---

[3] Examples from *Modern Spanish*, 2nd ed., by Bolinger *et al.*, p. 194, © 1960, 1966, by Harcourt, Brace & World, Inc., and reprinted with their permission.

1. Repetition drill.

In this drill, students repeat individually or in chorus exactly what has been modelled. We use this drill especially for dialogue presentation or for the establishment of a new pattern.

Teacher (model)	**Estamos en casa.**
Students (echo)	**Estamos en casa.**
Teacher (model)	**Estoy en casa.**
Students (echo)	**Estoy en casa.**
Teacher (model)	**Está en casa.**
Students (echo)	**Está en casa.**

2. Combination drill.

In this drill, two independent clauses are compressed (or combined) into a single sentence.

Teacher (model)	**La muchacha se pone el abrigo. La muchacha es inteligente.**
Students (echo)	**La muchacha se pone el abrigo. La muchacha es inteligente.**
Teacher (cue)	(hand signal)
Students (respond)	**La muchacha inteligente se pone el abrigo.**
(or)	**La muchacha que se pone el abrigo es inteligente.**

3. Rejoinder drill.

There are two types of rejoinder drills: directed rejoinder and free rejoinder. In the former, the student is told what he is to do (directed dialogue). In the latter, the student is free to respond in any stylistically appropriate manner.

A. Directed rejoinder drill:

Teacher	**Pablo, pregúntele a Juan qué hizo durante las vacaciones.**
First Student	**Juan, ¿qué hiciste durante las vacaciones?**
Teacher	**Juan, dígale que fue de viaje.**
Second Student	**Fui de viaje.**

B. Free rejoinder drill:

Teacher **Me duelen los pies.**

Student _____ (Here he might answer
"Qué lástima!," **"Lo
siento,"** or whatever is
appropriate)

4. Question formation drill.

Especially useful in Spanish, where word order is affected by inter-
rogation, is the drill in which we teach the student to form a question
from a declarative cue.

Teacher (cue) **Juan** compró un libro para su hermana ayer.
Student ¿Quién compró un libro para su hermana ayer?

Teacher Juan compró **un libro** para su hermana ayer.
Student ¿Qué compró Juan para su hermana ayer?

To be successful, drills impose two requirements, the first having to
do with their preparation, the second with their use. As to preparation,
it must be emphasized again that there is no substitute for drills prepared under the guidance of a trained linguist and double-checked for
idiomatic authenticity by a native speaker. Whenever possible, traditional materials should be discarded in favor of audio-lingual materials. Where it is impossible to do so, and the teacher wishes to update
his traditional text, it is always wiser to adapt drills from prepared
audio-lingual materials (cf. bibliography at end of Chapter 2). The
teacher inexperienced in drill-making must proceed with caution in
creating his own drills until he has had the opportunity to practice
extensively under critical guidance.

As to how best to use the drills, we must remember that it is vital
that every student participate. The beauty of audio-lingual drills is
their adaptability to either choral or individual recitation, and we must
take advantage of this to make sure that everyone takes part. The fact
that a drill has only eight items in no way limits it to eight individuals
in the class. It is always assumed that a drill will be repeated over and
over until every student has a chance to vary all the slots requested to
be changed. The object of these drills (as is the object of all audio-
lingual drills) is fluency. The drill is to be repeated until the entire class
can perform it flawlessly (and with an authentic accent). In some
classes, an exercise will be performed perfectly after only a few minutes

of practice. In others, nearly half a period must be spent on a relatively brief exercise. Only the perfect performance of a drill indicates that the drill has ended. Class time can be saved, of course, by having the student practice the drills ahead of time in the language laboratory.

We shall have more to say about the additional uses to which these drills may be put in our chapter on the language laboratory. For a somewhat technical explanation of the grammatical principles which underlie these drill types, the interested student may consult the works listed in the bibliography for this chapter.

▶ EXERCISES

1. Describe the following drills in terms of progressive or simple sub-stitution or correlation, noting if expansion, replacement, alteration, or reduction is involved. Where these terms are not applicable, indicate the drill's purpose and attempt to describe it according to the principles involved.

   (a) *Patterned response drill*

   > ¿Estudia Ud. el español? _____
   > ¿Busca Ud. los libros? _____
   > ¿Conoce Ud. a Luisa? _____
   > ¿Quiere Ud. las papas fritas? _____

   (b) *Choice question-response drill*

   > Cuando Ud. estaba en España, ¿comía en casa o iba a un café?
   > ¿Cuál de las corbatas prefieres, la negra o la verde?
   > ¿Vuelve Ud. a las ocho o las nueve?
   > ¿Le parece este señor inteligente o tonto?

   (c) *Translation Drill* [4]

   > **Hace poco que lo vi durmiendo.**
   > I saw him eating a short time ago.
   > I saw him reading a short time ago.
   > I saw him waiting a long time ago.
   > I saw him sleeping a long time ago.
   > I saw him running an hour ago.
   > I saw him working a week ago.

---

[4] From *A-LM Spanish*, (First Edition) *Level One*, p. 135, © 1960 by Harcourt, Brace & World, Inc., and reprinted with their permission.

(d) *Translation review drill* [5]

Me parece que es americana.
I think she is American.
I think she speaks Spanish.
It seems to me she is Spanish.
It seems to me she speaks English.
She says no.

(e) *Combined pattern replacement drill* [6]

Nosotros queremos invitarlo al cine.

			fiesta.
____	llevarla	____	
			tienda.
____	ir	____	
____	prefieres	____	
			hospital.
Nosotros	____		
			cena.

2. Explain how the concept of individual co-occurrence and construction co-occurrence affects the way in which drills are constructed.
3. How can a cue (the phrase said by the teacher to stimulate the student's response) be presented so that not more than one slot is potentially filled at any given stage of the drill? Construct brief sample drills to illustrate the right and wrong ways.
4. Use the following three phrases as basic frames. Construct a simple substitution drill for Frame A, using slots 1 and 2. Do the same for Frame B, using slots 1, 2, and 3. Construct a simple correlation drill for Frame C.

FRAME	BASIC PATTERN SENTENCE
A	**Pedro se sienta.**
B	**Eliseo habla chino.**
C	**Anastasio es polaco.**

REFERENCE BOOKS AND ARTICLES

BELASCO, SIMON. "Introduction" in *Applied Linguistics: Spanish* (Boston: D. C. Heath, 1961), pp. i–xxxix.

[5] Adapted from Bolinger *et al.*, *op. cit.*, p. 282.
[6] From *A-LM Spanish*, *op. cit.*, p. 72.

BOWEN, J. DONALD and ROBERT P. STOCKWELL. *The Structures of English and Spanish* (Chicago: University of Chicago Press, 1965).

KENISTON, HAYWARD. *Spanish Syntax List* (New York: Holt, 1937).

CRIADO DEL VAL, MANUEL. *Gramática española* (Madrid: Editorial SAETA, 1958).

GRAVIT, FRANCIS W. and ALBERT VALDMAN, eds. "Structural Drills and the Language Laboratory," Report of the Third Language Laboratory Conference, Indiana University, March 1962. (*International Journal of American Linguistics* XXVIII, Part II, April 1963).

HUGHES, JOHN P. *Linguistics and Language Teaching* (New York: Random House, 1968).

MOULTON, WILLIAM G. "What is Structural Drill?" (*International Journal of American Linguistics* XXIX, 1963), 3–15.

O'CONNOR, PATRICIA *et al. Oral Drill in Spanish*, 2nd ed. (Boston: Houghton Mifflin, 1963).

PALERMO, JOSEPH A. "A Direct Look at Spanish Grammar" (*Hispania* XXXV, 1952), 399–406.

POLITZER, ROBERT L. and CHARLES N. STAUBACH. *Teaching Spanish: A Linguistic Orientation*, rev. ed. (Waltham, Mass.: Blaisdell, 1965).

STACK, EDWARD M. *The Language Laboratory and Modern Language Teaching*, rev. ed. (New York: Oxford University Press, 1966).

TWADDELL, W. F. "Meanings, Habits and Rules" (*Language Learning* II, 1949), 4–11.

6

The language laboratory

Much of the current interest in foreign language programs in the secondary school centers around the language laboratory. The laboratory has almost simultaneously been touted as a panacea for all types of language learning problems and denounced as useless, once the student loses interest in the "novelty" of the mechanical devices employed in the lab. A realistic view, as we might expect, is somewhere between these two extremes. As most linguists with experience in dealing with beginning language studies will agree, the laboratory is not the only way to gain proficiency in a language. The fundamental skills approach does not depend entirely upon the laboratory for its success, although its effectiveness is generally enhanced by using the lab. While many of us as language teachers have had good students who do not use, and apparently do not need to use, laboratory facilities to acquire proficiency, evidence also indicates that the low-aptitude (yet motivated) student will gain much from the use of the laboratory program, often exceeding, by hard work and concentrated laboratory practice, the achievements of high-aptitude students.

The laboratory, like the audio-lingual approach itself, is largely the product of experience gained in the World War II Army language training programs. In these programs, which we discussed in Chapter 1, the learning of a foreign language was treated as the acquisition of particular skills, which could be acquired only through the "overlearning" of material until it became a part of the learner's automatic speech habits. This was accomplished by intensive practice sessions in which dialogues and pattern drills were done and redone under the supervision of a native-speaking instructor. As this amount of student-teacher contact was impossible in the school systems, the laboratory was seen as one way to provide this guided, programmed instruction without the physical presence of the teacher. The laboratory in today's secondary school serves to help the student assimilate speech patterns by overlearning until they become his own habits of expression. In this sense, the student has, in a self-contained listener-speaker situation, the opportunity for audio-lingual practice and aural experience with authentic materials.

Because the student in the language laboratory is isolated both from his group and from external distractions, he is able to give maximum attention to the taped materials. This individualized experience also makes the student less self-conscious when he is required to repeat after the tape, reducing the inhibition factor so detrimental to effective language learning.

Another physical advantage of the laboratory is that the student is able to speak individually for an entire laboratory period, whereas in class each student is fortunate to speak for a minute or two in a whole hour (except in repetition drills, etc., of course). This is making efficient use of the student's time since he is spending every minute in active production of language.

Psychologically, the laboratory is an "all-business" environment and in some cases actually increases the attentiveness of some students. We might also mention that a well-equipped language laboratory provides the student with high fidelity sound reproduction through his earphones, free from external interference to which he is subjected in class, including the inevitable influence of the imperfect pronunciation of adjacent students. Although it is a good idea, as the student advances, to expose him to muffled speech or noisy environments to accustom him to everyday speech situations in which street noises and the like do "blur" conversation, beginning and intermediate students will profit from the clear reproduction of the acoustic image by high-fidelity equipment.

The student is allowed to proceed at his own optimum rate of learning by the procedure of self-pacing with programmed laboratory materials. Thus the laboratory is also a way for students to make up an occasional lesson missed due to absence, or to provide the superior student with the opportunity to work ahead with greater challenge.

Because the language laboratory is still a somewhat revolutionary phenomenon in language teaching, not all teachers agree as to how it should be used, what goals should be set for it, what results can be expected, and how the teacher's responsibilities toward it should be distributed. Consequently, a new methodology has been developed (or rather, is evolving) toward finding ways to couple this radically different teaching device to the older ones with which we are already familiar.

Is the laboratory simply a classroom with electronic equipment? No, the laboratory has its own set of functions which it performs in addition to, and not in place of, the regular classroom teaching program. Misuses of the laboratory are due in part to misunderstandings concerning its proper role and to a less than complete consideration of all the implications of these functions.

As a collection of equipment the laboratory does nothing by itself, and because it is at its weakest when superimposed on traditional instructional practice, it is vital that the physical layout of the laboratory and its position in the foreign language program in each school be considered as inseparable. The prime voice in the final decisions about purchase, design, staffing, scheduling, and materials should be that of the foreign language faculty of the school concerned. From the outset, matters of staffing the laboratory and keeping it open at the times when it will best serve the needs of the program of which it is an integral part are as urgent an issue at the planning stage as the selection of the electro-mechanical equipment itself (cf. items 1 through 9 in the *Do's and Don't's* at the end of this chapter).

Since, as we have said, the purpose of the laboratory is to provide the student with the practice he needs to make the patterns he has learned a part of his speech habits, only material which has first been presented to him and subjected to the teacher's correction in class is fit material for the laboratory. This does not mean that material which is a variation on that presented in class (such as recombination narratives of dialogue materials, as discussed in Chapter 3) is not proper laboratory fare, but rather that the laboratory is not the place for the presentation of new material. Indeed, the very selection of the basic classroom textbook should be strongly influenced by whether or not it is designed not only to develop the listening and speaking skills, but also to integrate class and laboratory work.

The class drills and their counterparts in the laboratory should be designed so as to accent especially the points of conflict between the source and target languages. Everything that is new to the student, suggests George Scherer,[1] should be brought to the "safety level" in class first by the teacher before the students are sent to the laboratory

---

[1] George A. C. Scherer, "The Use and Misuse of the Language Laboratory" (*German Quarterly* XXXVIII, May 1965) 335–344.

for overlearning the same material. The safety level is that level of accomplishment which insures that every student is hearing what he should be hearing, and that he is echoing the material accurately, not only in chorus, but alone.

Recordings of songs, plays, and recitations are useful in the laboratory only when the student is already familiar with the vocabulary and structure patterns which form the basis of these materials. (It is understood, of course, that the student is expected to be able to induce meanings and functions from familiar vocabulary and structure items.) Very few teachers give their students enough listening practice and articulatory correction before exposing them to laboratory work.

Pierre Delattre [2] suggests that there are three goals for which language laboratories were created: (1) to develop natural speed in conversational response, without reflection as to the grammar rules involved; (2) to learn the patterns of a language orally, without reference to a spelling that would mask the linguistic truth; and (3) to acquire habits of correct pronunciation and fluent aural comprehension.

The function of the laboratory then is to supplement the classroom procedure by providing the student with an opportunity for extensive, planned, individual practice with authentic materials, once these materials have been carefully presented and drilled in the classroom. In this sense, the idea that every classroom should be at once a classroom and a laboratory (the so-called electronic classroom) is neither necessary nor even recommended as long as the laboratory is made available to the students for extra practice along lines we shall suggest below.

Despite a great deal of literature which tends to dispute the principle of the language laboratory as a supplementary program, the vast majority of experts in the field adhere to the approach we are supporting. The obvious implication in the concept of the laboratory as an adjunct to the classroom is that it is to be used beyond the language class hours. This does not mean that it is entirely an after-school arrangement, for it is possible to make the laboratory available during the lunch hour and those hours when students, in many schools at least, have the opportunity to decide about the wise use of their time during certain "free" periods.

Certainly the laboratory can be nothing more than a novelty for the students as long as the once- or twice-weekly migration system (classroom to laboratory and back), or the mistaken use of the laboratory as a classroom is tolerated. It is wasteful to pre-empt the teacher's

---

[2] Pierre Delattre, "Testing Audio Equipment by Ear" (*Audiovisual Instruction*, 5, May 1960), 156.

time pushing buttons instead of teaching. These negative practices are due, in part, to the difficult problem of scheduling so that appropriate outside-of-class use of the laboratory would be possible.

There is no easy way around it — there will be extra hours of work required for the effective use of the laboratory, and released time for a teacher or the use of a teacher-aide must be planned from the outset.

The equipment to be found in secondary school laboratories varies with the use that the school plans for it and with the funds available for the purchase of equipment. This is an extremely serious matter in that if the equipment does not fully meet the exact specifications of the program in which it is to be used, it can easily ruin that program. Fundamental to all effective installations is this dual need: (1) the student must be able to listen to, and (2) to record his own voice. Less necessary but still desirable is a monitoring device so that the teacher can, if he chooses, listen in on his students as they practice.

To be effective in its role as a supplementary practice center, the laboratory must be a room separate and distinct from the classroom. The concept of the electronic classroom, which doubles as laboratory and classroom, is often erroneously viewed as a means of eliminating a separate language laboratory with resulting financial economies. But if we compare the four major functions of the electronic classroom [(1) the immediate shifting from live to tape presentation and back, as in dialogue presentations; (2) the immediate accessibility of a native model of dialogue and drill material in the text; (3) the conservation of the teacher's voice in certain kinds of drills; (4) the limited testing of listening comprehension] with what can be accomplished in the laboratory, we realize that the electronic classroom may be a desirable adjunct to, but never a replacement for, a well-designed laboratory.

We shall only outline here some of the more universal features of the efficient laboratory. The teacher may consult the references given at the end of this chapter for more detailed information, remembering that it is not the size of the laboratory but rather the quality of the equipment it contains that ultimately determines its value.

We divide the laboratory into three main sections:

I. Administrative
   A. Master console
   B. Repair and maintenance counter
   C. Supervisor's desk and master tape storage unit

II. Instructional
   A. Student booths
   B. Library shelves for student tapes

III. Preparational — Recording studio

Let us now consider each of these sections in the light of the fore-going discussion. First, the administrative area. The master console, in addition to the master power switch for the whole laboratory, should also provide for:

1. playing a particular recorded program to any number or combination of student positions without necessarily preempting all positions;
2. dubbing several copies of tapes from the master played from the console to decks in the student booths;
3. monitoring any given student position while it is in use.

The monitoring function is actually optional, since monitoring is a technique with an unconvincing history of success. After all, teacher time is more profitably spent in the classroom. Only one booth can be monitored by a single person at one time, and the amount of attention thus given each student is relatively insignificant. Besides, it is often quite unnerving for the student suddenly to hear his program — to which he is supposedly paying close attention — abruptly interrupted by the voice of the unseen monitoring teacher.[3]

The laboratory testing program, more fully discussed in Chapter 8, does not, as is commonly held, depend upon monitoring facilities. Both auditory discrimination and comprehension tests make use of prepared answer sheets which provide the teacher with the raw data for evaluation and grading. Student responses in speaking tests are recorded in their entirety, and it is this tape which is evaluated by the teacher. Monitoring for testing purposes suffers from the same kind of inadequacies as does monitoring in its other phases: it is normally impossible to monitor individual students long enough or at comparable intervals during the laboratory session to achieve a truly accurate comparative evaluation.

If we eliminate the monitoring function, the master console should contain one or more playback machines (for dubbing or generating a master program), a disc turntable and pickup, a master microphone which can replace any other program source at any time, and program selector switches which allow the teacher or supervisor to control the distribution when more than one program source is in use. A small workbench with a locked cabinet should be provided for the repair of minor breakdowns. A desk, locked file, and bulletin board should be

---

[3] For a further discussion of monitoring, see H. E. Probyn, "The Role of the Monitor in the Language Laboratory" (*Audio-Visual Language Journal* III, 1966), 137–141.

provided for the laboratory supervisor. A large locked cabinet should also be provided in the administrative area for the storage of master and virgin tapes.

The instructional area consists primarily of student positions. These should be booths with acoustically treated side panels, glass front, and open back (where the student sits). The transparent front is important so that the supervisor can see any student at work at any time. Each booth should be equipped with facilities for the student to hear the program, respond to it, and either hear his response simultaneously or record it for playback comparison, and to control the rate of presentation of the program by lengthening the pauses in it.

The equipment might ideally consist of a headset-microphone combination, a two-track record-playback tape deck with individual volume and on/off controls, and a pause pedal. Although no one student may put all these facilities to use at a given moment, we feel that the well-designed laboratory will provide all the features we are describing if it is to achieve maximum flexibility and effectiveness. The headset-microphone plus the record-playback equipment at each student booth provide the possibilities of audio-passive, audio-active, and audio-active-evaluative learning experiences. *Audio-passive* refers to equipment which provides only facilities for listening; *audio-active* adds the possibility of the student's hearing his own voice through the earphones in response to the stimuli; *audio-active-evaluative* indicates equipment which includes the foregoing plus the possibility of the student recording his response for immediate or delayed playback and comparison.

The pause control adds the important dimension of self-pacing essential to individual programmed work in a library-style laboratory.

The master console, as we have described it, provides for the predetermined pacing of a given program in any one booth, combination of booths, or all booths.

The accessibility of open shelves where student tapes are available for the particular program used in the foreign language sequence and for supplementary work guarantees maximum realization of the laboratory's use potential without adding the "check in/check out" task to the supervisor's duties.

The recording "studio" is, at best, a separate, soundproof room with a highly sensitive microphone and recording equipment with which the foreign language faculty may prepare new teaching materials. Where a separate room is not possible, a well-insulated student-type booth with the appropriate recording equipment may be substituted.

The laboratory room itself should be acoustically treated, well lighted and ventilated, and appropriately wired.

In the planning of all these features, the foreign language faculty should seek the aid of a qualified consultant not committed to the interests of any single equipment manufacturer. The consultant must be a specialist in language laboratory construction and use; the local physics teacher or audio-visual technician is rarely sufficiently trained in these specific areas of concern to function adequately as consultant.

In addition to these features, the laboratory should also contain facilities for the projection of motion pictures and slides, for the display of visual aids, and for the overhead projection of opaque materials and transparencies.

Material for use in the laboratory is usually divided into two types: (1) pre-recorded, commercially produced tapes to accompany particular textbooks; and (2) tapes recorded by individual teachers or specially hired native speakers to supplement course work. Because these tapes serve the students as models of diction, it is imperative that they be of excellent acoustic quality and spoken by native (or near-native) speakers whose voices reveal pleasing quality, ample range, and extremely clear pronunciation. The greater the variety of accents and voice types represented on the tapes, as long as they are unquestionably authentic, the better, since the variations will help prepare the student for the natural variations encountered in the countries where the target language is spoken.

Directions to the student on how to use the tapes are clearest when presented in three phases: (1) as part of the assignment given in the classroom, (2) on a written sheet which the student either keeps in his notebook or which is given to him as he enters the laboratory, and (3) repeated at the beginning of the tape. These directions should be clear and succinct. Where they are unusually long or complex, they should be repeated. Students should be given sufficient time, also, to adjust to the directions; this sometimes calls for pauses within the recorded instructions. If the tape consists of exercises to be done in conjunction with a text, the page, paragraph, and line numbers should be given. Students and laboratory technicians always appreciate knowing exactly where specific exercises end. A simple "End of Exercise X," said on the tape is generally sufficient.

Among other technical considerations before making tapes is one of time. Since the laboratory is essentially a device for reinforcement, optimum results are obtained when the assignments are relatively brief and intensive. A tape which can be repeated three times during the laboratory period is considered to be of adequate length. Time is also an important factor in exercises which the student is asked to repeat after a model. To allow for the pupil's hesitation and slower rate of reproduction, the pauses allowed for his repetition should be approximately 30%–50% longer than the time it took for the model to record the utterance. Sometimes a cue, such as a click or a snap, will speed up the pupil's response.

The content of tapes depends largely upon the needs of the students, but is also determined by the fact that the language laboratory is most effective in promoting speaking and comprehension skills. Drills to improve pronunciation and intonation may be specially devised for the production of individual sounds, sound sequences, or intonation patterns. Taped exercises on individual sound problems, such as accompany many texts, are helpful in focusing the pupils' attention on specific pronunciation problems; but it is well to remember that pronunciation and intonation accuracy will also be improved through laboratory practice with the structural patterns from dialogues or pattern practice sessions.

Special precautions are needed in the early months when students have not yet acquired the awareness necessary to recognize subtle discrepancies between the model and their reproduction of it. For this reason, early laboratory assignments are best limited exclusively to duplicating rather than expanding material already presented in class. Later, as students learn to discriminate, they may train themselves in self-monitoring which is, after all, a major goal of laboratory practice.

The basic format of all laboratory tapes which is adhered to by the best commercially produced materials and which should be scrupulously observed by persons creating new materials for use in the laboratory is as follows:

1. The exercises on the tapes are designed to make the pupil either echo — that is, imitate — what he has heard, or to make him respond — in other words, create the new grammatical pattern requested.
2. The listen-and-respond exercises work on the Skinnerian principle of Stimulus-Response-Reinforcement.[4] That is, the pupil first hears a stimulus, such as a word or a sentence. Then there is a pause in which he is to say what is requested of him. Immediately afterward he hears the correct response so that he may know at once whether he was right or wrong. Then the model echoes the correct response for reinforcement. Finally, a new stimulus is presented.

---

[4] The application of the Skinnerian principle as stated here has been evolved by Gustave Mathieu.

Cycle 1	Cycle 2	Cycle 3	Cycle 4	Cycle 5	Cycle 1
Stimulus.	Pause for learner to respond.	Correct response.	Pause for learner to echo.	Model echoes correct response to leave the pupil with the correct acoustic image.	etc.

Cycle 2. If a strictly controlled space for the student's response is required, then the appropriate space must be provided on the tape. However, if a response to be made at a specific rate of speed is not required, then no space is provided on tape, but rather merely an auditory signal (bell or buzzer) sounds to indicate that the student should activate the pause control to provide enough time to form the correct response.

Cycle 4. Here again, if no space has been provided on the tape for the student's echo, then as soon as he has listened to the correct response in Cycle 3, he activates the pause control again while *echoing* the correct response. If the pupil responded correctly in Cycle 2, repeating the response in Cycle 4 will reinforce his mastery of the pattern. If, however, he has said it incorrectly, echoing the correct response will help him learn it.

3. After completing the first practice using the pause control, the pupil rewinds the tape and goes through the exercise again *without* the pause control. This will help build up speech reflexes to the point of automaticity that comes only with much practice. The pupil should go over the drill again and again until he can do it perfectly and correctly in the pause provided on the tape. Once the pupil has mastered each item, it should not take him any longer to make his responses than the time provided on the tape.

The teacher should, as a general practice, listen to all tapes to be used as laboratory assignments so that he may eliminate from his own modelling of the utterances which the student will later use in the laboratory, any disparity between his oral production and that of the taped model.

Syntactic drills, like the phonetic drills we have been discussing, are best suited for laboratory purposes when the target item is not long and remains predictably consistent throughout the exercise. Thus, almost all of the pattern-drill types discussed in Chapter 5 are potentially useful for the laboratory. Translation drills, combined pattern replacement drills, and free rejoinder drills are better reserved exclusively for classroom use. Exactly as in the creation of classroom drills, a sufficient amount of context should surround the target item; the resulting target change should represent only the desired variation. Concise drills, scheduled so that the entire tape can be done at least three times in a given laboratory period, will produce the best results.

In addition to pronunciation and syntactic drills, oral-aural comprehension-reproduction drills are useful in the laboratory. In these exercises, designed for more advanced pupils, narrative phrases demonstrating more subtle pronunciation and intonation patterns, conditioned by longer and more complex sentences, are presented for repetition. The student repeats without benefit of written text. For the purposes of such drills, tapes can be prepared from existing recordings of contemporary theater or from class materials. Dialogue from the theater is always the preferred literary form for audio-lingual drills since it comes closest to normal speech. Poetry is discouraged since formal poetic recitation is not usually representative of standard speech. Again, these materials should be introduced only after the basic structure and vocabulary contained have been presented in class.

The development of an accurate and meaningful testing program for the language laboratory is a continuing concern. Only recently have successful tests been devised to correspond to the two skills that may best be developed in the laboratory: listening-comprehension and speaking. We shall discuss the construction of specific tests in Chapter 8. Our purpose below is merely to describe the most successful areas of testing which may be carried out in the laboratory.

Tests of speaking ability should parallel as closely as possible the format of laboratory lessons. That is, the test must require the student to make spoken responses to auditory or visual stimuli at a rate of speed which, while permitting him sufficient time to respond, does not allow time for reflection about the grammar rules involved. Pattern drills are in themselves, as we have mentioned, speaking tests, in that they are done orally. In this sense they make good foundations for laboratory tests. It might be added that a speaking test should always include a part specifically covering correct pronunciation and intonation. Again, the same pronunciation drill format from daily laboratory lessons will serve as an adequate test, provided that the scope of the drill-test is broad enough to include all the necessary material.

Some schools have found laboratory testing to be impractical, and have abandoned it in favor of personal interviews, including aural-oral sections in regular classroom tests or using a tape recorder in the classroom. Bolinger suggests several important drawbacks to laboratory testing which should be eliminated or compensated for before proceeding. Among them are, first, the fact that not all students are equally adept at manipulating laboratory machinery introduces the extraneous factor of manual dexterity into the test. Second, there is the question of mechanical failure which, even in the case of a single position, can invalidate an entire test. Third, laboratory tests, in which everybody is required to say the same answer at the same time, create a confusing din and also may permit the unprepared student to overhear the correct answer from his neighbor, thus invalidating the examination as a reliable evaluation of what that student knows.

Scheduling students for laboratory sessions, both during the school day and after school, is a difficult matter, and one that can be resolved, as we have said, only as each institution takes into account the number of positions available, the length of the school day, the number of students required to use the laboratory, the length of the laboratory session itself, the availability of technical assistants and faculty supervisors, etc. Some researchers feel that laboratory sessions of more than thirty minutes each are counterproductive, in that the attention span of most pupils does not exceed thirty minutes of intensive drill. Sloppy work in the laboratory, of course, encourages the habituation of inaccurate responses, so care should be exercised not to overload the pupil in the laboratory. It is generally advisable to insist that all students make use of the laboratory for a specified length of time each day. This avoids the punitive atmosphere that has evolved in some schools in which "better" students are exempted from laboratory exercises.

Tape loan programs have helped many institutions solve some of their scheduling problems. The program involves dubbing the master tape for a given practice session on a pupil's own tape. In many districts enough students have access to a tape recorder at home to make this a practical way of increasing listening time and cutting down the load on the laboratory itself. It is cheaper to dub a tape than to install additional positions.

Precautions must be taken, however, regarding the use of copyrighted materials in the laboratory and making them available for dubbing. Although many schools do lend tapes by considering them extensions of the laboratory exercises, it is well to secure direct information from the publishers concerning your school's rights in dubbing and loaning tapes.

Detailed suggestions for day-to-day procedures for operating the laboratory and for the ordering, recording, dubbing, labelling, and storing of tapes will be found in the sources referred to in the bibliography and appendices at the end of this chapter. Computerized laboratories and installations which provide as well for visual components for programmed learning are now coming into use, and the reader will want to investigate and keep abreast of these new developments in the current professional literature.

Planning and Operating a Language Lab or an Electronic Classroom in a High School: A Dozen Do's and Don't's

1. DO hire a consultant (not employed by a lab equipment manufacturer), to help you plan, evaluate bids, do the final checking of installed equipment.

1. DON'T try to do it yourself; planning a lab requires as much knowledge as planning a school *and* a radio station.

2. DO define your teaching objectives first and then choose equipment that will implement them.

2. DON'T leave the planning entirely to administrators or A-V specialists, who may know little about foreign language teaching.

3. DO see at least three different types of successful installations in operation before you decide on your equipment.

3. DON'T plan a lab for use by everyone (foreign languages, English, shorthand, speech); this will result in confusion and frustration.

4. DO follow the instructions and guidelines (pp. 26–28, 263–287) in the Council of Chief State School Officers' *Purchase Guide* (Ginn and Co., 1959) and its *Supplement* (Ginn and Co., 1961).

4. DON'T forget that a lab is no stronger than its weakest component, mechanical or human.

5. DO urge each teacher who is to use the lab to study the growing literature on the subject and take a workshop course.

5. DON'T expect the foreign language teacher to teach and operate the lab at the same time; hire a technician to assist him.

6. DO write exact specifications into your contract and accept delivery as completed only when the equipment tests up to specifications and functions smoothly for a full month and when there are adequate provisions for servicing.

6. DON'T forget Murphy's Law of Electronics: Anything that *can* go wrong *will*.

7. DO build an expandable and flexible lab to handle future increases in demand and improvements in equipment and methods.

7. DON'T overlook the alternative of electronic equipment in each foreign language classroom instead of a single lab.

8. DO provide for regular preventive maintenance, with an annual budget of 3% to 5% of your total initial cost.

8. DON'T forget to budget for tapes, discs, and other expendable equipment.

9. DO insist that the lab work be an integral part of the foreign language course.

9. DON'T impose the lab program on unwilling or unprepared foreign language teachers; start with one beginning course taught by an enthusiast, make it a success, then add other courses one at a time.

10. DO plan for short lab sessions; twenty minutes of active daily use is the ideal.

10. DON'T expect *all* your equipment to function all the time; provide 10% to 20% spare parts or use only 80% to 90% capacity.

11. DO arrange your seating and equipment with provision for viewing as well as hearing and speaking.

11. DON'T accept inferior sound; tapes should be free of extraneous noise, and capable of producing sounds as natural and full-ranged as a live voice.

12. DO cut in half the teaching load of the lab director and allow released time for all teachers who prepare lab materials.

12. DON'T expect the lab to reduce the teacher's work; it will increase it, redistribute it, reorient it, and make it more effective.[5]

Job Description: Duties of Language Laboratory Supervisor
by Gustave Mathieu

GENERAL.

1. Works under the direct supervision of the Chairman, Department of Foreign Languages.
2. Assists foreign language teachers by operating equipment, locating materials, and playing tapes and records as requested.
3. Helps train inexperienced, new, substitute, and student teachers in the use of laboratory equipment.
4. Performs clerical tasks related to the laboratory.

---

[5] *A Dozen Do's and Don't's for Planning and Operating a Language Lab or an Electronic Classroom in a High School* (New York: MLA Materials Center, 1961).

5. Advises when supplies and materials should be ordered and when it may be necessary to repair or replace items of equipment.
6.. Keeps laboratory open before and after school for work by individual students (absentees, slow students, gifted students, etc.).

SPECIFIC.

1. Opens language laboratory and closes it at designated time.
2. Plans and maintains a daily work sheet.
3. Operates tape recorders and record players used in the laboratory.
4. Places tapes and records on players according to requests of instructors and students using the language laboratory.
5. Prepares equipment for use by instructors and students.
6. Checks and examines players, earphones, and microphones before each lab period to insure that they are in good working condition.
7. Makes copies of instructor-made tapes, duplicates commercial materials (when permitted), and accumulates individual student recordings on tapes; cuts, splices, and repairs tapes, inserting leaders and labelling properly.
8. Catalogues, files, issues, receives, and maintains tapes, records, scripts, and other instructional materials and supplies.
9. Keeps records of location and use of instructional materials.
10. Types and maintains lists, inventories, schedules, charts, and similar records.
11. Checks attendance of students.
12. Cleans earphones and microphones frequently.
13. Maintains and makes minor repairs to equipment used in the laboratory; cleans, demagnetizes, and lubricates tape heads, guides and runners; cleans capstans and guides, lubricates motors in tape decks as recommended by manufacturer; polishes heads; checks and replaces needles on turntable arms; checks and replaces rubber drive belts; adjusts speed for tape decks; cleans and dusts equipment. Calls repairman for major repairs.
14. Turns off power and locks all equipment, windows, and doors before leaving for the day.
15. Performs other work as required.[6]

Useful Accessories for Making Tapes
by Gustave Mathieu

1. *Leader and Timing Tape.* Splice two to three feet to each end of the tape. Leader tape protects against damage and breakage to

---

[6] A more detailed analysis of the responsibilities of the supervisor of a modern language laboratory will be found in Daymond Turner, "Occupation: Language Laboratory Director" (*Modern Language Journal* XLVIII, 3, 1964) 151–154.

the ends of the tape. It also permits recording to the very end of the tape and starting at a precise point. Leader tape can also be inserted between selections for easy identification. Lastly, pertinent data (speed, selection, etc.) can be written on the leader tape with pen or pencil.

2. *Splicing Tape.* Do not use ordinary cellophane tape for splicing. Use only splicing tape.

3. *Automatic Tape Splicer.* Will permit splicing tape quickly, easily, and professionally.

4. *A Pair of Scissors.* For cutting tape. Keep scissors unmagnetized.

5. *Self-Adhesive Labels.* To identify a reel of tape in case it becomes separated from its jacket. Use self-sticking label.

6. *Pen or Pencil.* To write data on the stick-on label and the jacket. (Selection, course, length or playing time, speed, date, etc.).

7. *Bookstand.* For easier reading of script while recording.

8. *Patch Cord.* For transferring material from one tape to another or from record to tape.

9. *Stop Watch.* An important accessory for timing tape or individual selections and pauses for echo or response by students. It should have a stop-and-start button in case there are interruptions while recording the tape.

10. *Bulk Eraser.* For erasing a recorded tape in a few seconds without having to run it through the tape recorder.

11. "Recording — Do Not Disturb" sign.

Tips for Making a Good Master Tape

by Gustave Mathieu

1. Always work from a written script. Rehearse script before recording.

2. Bring the microphone as close as possible to the mouth — within two to four inches.

3. Make sure that the recording indicator provides a good recording level, not too high and not too low.

4. Do not speak directly into microphone but past it. This will reduce the aspiration of voiceless stops like p and the hissing sound of sibilants like s.

5. Suspend microphone if possible or place it on separate table. This will prevent the microphone from picking up vibrations made by the tape recorder.

6. Place script on a reading stand. This avoids the necessity of lowering the head while speaking.

7. The microphone should be placed at least four feet from the nearest wall unless this wall is soundproofed.
8. Always work with a tape recorder that has an instantaneous pause button with lock. This will enable the speaker to stop and start the tape instantly without having to stop and restart the entire mechanism — but without recording a click.
9. Be sure to turn off fans or any other apparatus that may be picked up as background noise by the microphone.
10. When rewinding, remove tape from head.
11. Listen to the completed tape to check.

NOTE: A soundproofed recording cabin is most useful but not essential. One of its chief advantages is that the teacher will be able to make master tapes while other activities are going on in the laboratory or the school.

▶ EXERCISES

1. Why is taking a class to the laboratory for a given portion of the class period each day or two less profitable than making the lab assignment for an after-school or "free-hour" period, often in lieu of written homework?
2. Your district plans to spend $10,000 for electromechanical language teaching devices in your school. Your faculty is given its choice of three electronic classrooms or one audio-active-evaluative lab. Discuss the advantages and disadvantages of either of the alternatives.
3. Assuming that the laboratory has provisions for self-pacing, should a limitation be put on the fast learner to keep him from progressing rapidly without really having mastered each step along the way? How will good students, taking advantage of self-pacing to advance more rapidly, affect the rhythm of your classroom procedures? To what extent can the foregoing be considered a conclusive argument for or against a laboratory with provisions for self-pacing?
4. What arguments can you give for and against monitoring in the laboratory by the teacher?
5. What are the advantages of the audio-active-evaluative laboratory over one which is simply audio-active?
6. If you have a language laboratory in your school, describe it and the uses to which it is put, suggesting where it might be improved. If your school does not have one, discuss the problems involved in setting one up, scheduling its use, and programming materials for it.

BRIEF BIBLIOGRAPHY ON THE LANGUAGE LABORATORY
by Gustave Mathieu

ALLEN, EDWARD. "The Effects of the Language Laboratory on the Development of Skills in a Foreign Language" (*Modern Language Journal* XLIV, 1960), 355–358.

Audiovisual Instruction VII, November 1962. Special issue devoted to foreign language teachers.

BARRUTIA, RICHARD. "The Past, Present, and Future of Language Laboratories" (*Hispania* L, 1967), 875–887.

"Coordination Between Classroom and Laboratory," in *Reports of the Working Committees of the 1961 Northeast Conference on the Teaching of Foreign Languages*.

DELATTRE, PIERRE. "Testing Audio Equipment by Ear" (*Audiovisual Instruction* 5, May 1960), 156.

EDDY, FREDERICK D. and ELTON HOCKING, eds. *Purchase Guide for Programs in Science, Mathematics, Modern Foreign Languages* (Boston: Ginn and Co., 1959).
Supplement (Boston: Ginn and Co., 1961).

GRAVIT, FRANCIS W. and ALBERT VALDMAN, eds. *Structural Drills and the Language Laboratory*, Report of the Third Language Laboratory Conference held at Indiana University, March 1962, Bloomington, Indiana (*International Journal of American Linguistics* XXVIII, Part II, April 1963).

GRITTNER, FRANK and RUSSELL PAVLAT. *Language Laboratory Specifications* (Madison: Department of Public Instruction, 1965).

Guide for the Development of Language Laboratory Facilities. Bulletin of the California State Department of Education, Sacramento, Vol. 29, Oct. 1960.

HAYES, ALFRED S. *Technical Guide for Selection, Purchase, Use and Maintenance of Language Laboratory Facilities* (Washington, D.C.: USOE Bulletin OE–21024, 1963).

———. *Step-by-Step Procedures for Language Laboratory Planning: Some Suggestions for Schools and Colleges* (New York: MLA, 1960).

HEPWORTH, JOHN B. *The Language Laboratory. A Bibliography* (Manchester: Manchester Public Libraries, 1966).

HOCKING, ELTON. "Language Laboratories" (*The Nation's Schools* LXVII, February 1961).

———. *Language Laboratory and Language Learning* (Washington, D.C.: NEA, 1964).

———. "The Language Laboratory in Language Learning" (*California Schools* XXXI, January 1960), 33–34.

HOCKING, ELTON and ROBERT C. MERCHANT. "The Fabulous Language Labs" (*Educational Screen and Audio-Visual Guide* XXXVIII, April 1959), 184–187.

HUEBENER, THEODORE. *Audio-Visual Techniques in Teaching Foreign Languages* (New York: New York University Press, 1950).

HUTCHINSON, JOSEPH C. *Modern Foreign Languages in High Schools: The Language Laboratory* (Washington, D.C.: USOE, 1961).

———. *The Language Laboratory* (Washington, D.C.: Department of Health, Education and Welfare Bulletin OE–27013, 1961).

IODICE, DON. *Guidelines to Language Teaching in Classroom and Laboratory* (Electronic Teaching Laboratories, 1961).

JOHNSTON, MARJORIE C. and CATHERINE C. SEERLEY. *Foreign Language Laboratories in Schools and Colleges* (Washington, D.C.: USOE, 1959).

KONE, ELLIOTT H., ed. "Language Laboratories — Modern Techniques in Teaching Foreign Languages" (*Bulletin 19* of the Audio-Visual Education Association, Yale University Audio-Visual Center, 1959).

"Language Learning Today — 45 Questions and Answers" (*Audio-Visual Instruction*, Washington, D.C.: NEA, 1959).

LE BEL, C. J. *How to Make Good Tape Recordings* (New York: Audio-Devices, Inc., 1956).

LOCKE, WILLIAM H. "To Record or Not" (*Modern Language Journal* XLIV, October 1960).

———. "The Future of Language Laboratories" (*Modern Language Journal* XLIX, May 1965).

LORGE, SARAH W. "Language Laboratory Research Studies in New York City High Schools: A Discussion of the Program and the Findings" (*Modern Language Journal* XLVIII, November 1964).

MARK, DAVID. *How to Select and Use Your Tape Recorder* (New York: Rider, 1956).

MARTY, FERNAND L. *Language Laboratory Learning* (Wellesley: Audio-Visual Publications, 1960).

MATHIEU, GUSTAVE. "The Case for Tapes Without Pauses" (*Modern Language Journal* XLIX, January 1965).

———. "Language Laboratories" (*Review of Educational Research* XXXII, April 1962).

MORTON, F. RAND. "The Teaching Machine and the Teaching of Foreign Languages" (*PMLA* LXXV, 1960), 1–6.

NAJAM, EDWARD W. ed. *Materials and Techniques for the Language Laboratory*, Report of the Language Laboratory Conference held at Purdue University, March 1961, Bloomington, Indiana (*International Journal of American Linguistics* XXVIII, Part II, January 1962).

OINAS, FELIX J., ed. *Language Teaching Today*, Report of the Language Laboratory Conference held at Indiana University, January 1960, Bloomington, Indiana (*International Journal of American Linguistics* XXVI, Part II, October 1960).

Proceedings of the First Conference on the Role of the Language Laboratory in the Secondary Schools (Ann Arbor: University of Michigan Language Laboratory, 1960).

SÁNCHEZ, JOSÉ. "Twenty Years of Modern Language Laboratory: An Annotated Bibliography" (*Modern Language Journal* XLIII, 1959), 228–232.

SCHERER, GEORGE A. C. "The Use and Misuse of Language Laboratories" (*German Quarterly* XXXVIII, 1965), 335–341.

STACK, EDWARD M. *The Language Laboratory and Modern Language Teaching*, revised ed. (New York: Oxford University Press, 1966).

STAFFORD, THOMAS and ARTHUR KARKLINS. *First Aid for Tape Recorders* (Seattle: University of Washington, 1960).

WEILER, HAROLD. *Tape Recorders and Tape Recordings* (Mineola: Radio Magazines, Inc., 1956).

WEIR, RUTH HIRSCH. *Audio-Visual Aids in Language Teaching* (Washington, D.C.: Georgetown University, 1954).

WESTCOTT, CHARLES. *Tape Recorders, How They Work* (Indianapolis: H. W. Sams and Co., 1956).

7

Reading and writing in the audio-lingual approach

The skills of reading and writing a foreign language with comprehension and enjoyment, without reference to English, are skills which form an important part of foreign language education. The fundamental skills approach, despite a false impression to the contrary, does not eschew these skills but simply moves them to a different place in the sequence of learning. Furthermore, the fundamental skills approach re-evaluates the function of both these skills and has brought us new understanding of how much time should be devoted to teaching reading and writing and of what our goals should be.

The belief that skill in speaking the language is the only real measure of fluency leads the audio-lingual teacher to conclude that reading, whether it is basic or supplementary, must provide satisfaction to the learner. It may be undertaken as part of one's studies to gain information, for pleasure, or for an appreciation of literature or culture. In this sense, reading in the foreign language has the same general purpose as reading in the native language of the learner.

We have seen that the fundamental skills approach duplicates in its teaching program the order of steps in "natural" language learning: speak on the basis of what has already been heard; read on the basis of what has been heard and spoken; write on the basis of what has been heard, spoken, and read. Thus, it is only after the audio-lingual foundation has been laid that reading should be undertaken.

As Fries has pointed out, learning to read is learning to *do* something, and achievement in this skill should be evaluated on the efficiency of performance which can be achieved only through habit-forming practice.[1] Reading is a kind of linguistic response which depends upon the language control achieved by each particular individual reader and must therefore begin with, and build on, habits of language response already existing for the learner at that time.

The process of learning to read a language is the process of transfer from the auditory language signals, which have already been learned, to the new visual signs used to represent those same auditory signals, or the transfer from signals represented by auditory patterns to those same language signals represented by patterns of graphic shapes. One can "read" in so far as he can respond to the language signals, now represented by contrastive spelling patterns, as completely and efficiently as he has learned to respond to the same language signals formerly represented by the contrastive sound patterns.

Fries reminds the reader that this process of transfer is not the learning of the language code, nor is it the learning of a new or different set of language signals. It is not the learning of new "words", new grammatical structures, or new meanings. These are all language signals which the learner has mastered so well in the pre-reading phase of instruction that he is no longer conscious of their use. With more experience he will continue to develop his language capacity in the variety and number of lexical signals he can control. But this continual growth in meaning and in language signals must now draw attention away from the main business of the "transfer stage" of learning to read. During this period of learning to respond rapidly to the patterns of graphic shapes, the language materials used must be only those already well controlled audio-lingually by the pupil. The "transfer" stage is not the time to strive for the development of additional language mastery.

The learning of reading, then, consists primarily in recognizing graphic shapes in recurrent contrastive patterns and establishing a connection between these patterns and portions of the oral language signals. It is interesting to note, however, that written materials contain fewer language signals than does speech, for intonation, stress, and pause are not systematically represented in spelling. Fries suggests one sentence as an example of the many whose meaning changes with a different positioning of stress in speech, but which is not evident in the writing system:

---

[1] Charles C. Fries, *Linguistics and Reading* (New York: Holt, Rinehart and Winston, 1963), pp. 130 ff.

When did he *come?*
When did *he* come?
When *did* he come?
When did he come?

Productive reading, then, is achieved when the reader is able to supply those portions of significant language signals not represented graphically and to respond to them automatically. This is the second stage in reading, in which the graphic shapes themselves sink below the threshold of attention, and the reader is able to supply those portions of the signals which are not in the graphic representation.

The third stage begins when the reading process is so automatic that reading is used even more than the spoken language to stimulate vivid imagination and develop new experiences.

Reading may be intensive, extensive, or supplementary; oral or silent. By "intensive" reading is meant that the student not only comprehends the ideas of what he has read but also examines and studies new vocabulary and structure. "Extensive" reading minimizes detailed study and aims most often at reading for content. "Supplementary" reading involves the "extensive" reading of material related to cultural or linguistic information which arises in the study of the language itself. These supplementary readings are sometimes done in English in the early stages.

It stands to reason, then, that emphasis should be placed on intensive reading during the beginning semesters but should be decreased gradually as the student passes the third semester. By then, a general facility in reading simple texts should have been acquired and extensive reading can be introduced. By the final year (seventh and eighth semesters), the extensive and supplementary reading program becomes paramount and much of it is accomplished independently. Although many teachers successfully introduce some sight reading in the earlier semesters, this appears to be of only limited value.

The content of all reading material — for whatever purpose — should be linguistically and culturally authentic. Works in carelessly edited versions should be avoided from the very beginning. While it is often a good idea, in selecting reading material, to cater somewhat to the interests of students — to amuse them or to entertain them — this should never be done at the expense of linguistic or cultural authenticity.

The purpose of intensive reading is to develop the ability to understand the written foreign language without recourse to English. In this way, active vocabulary is reinforced and recognition vocabulary is increased. Besides, these early intensive readings build the pupil's appreciation of language patterns and style.

How do we introduce reading in the fundamental skills approach? Despite widely-held misconceptions, this approach generally initiates the students in intensive reading almost from the beginning. These initial readings are simply the same dialogues which form the core of the audio-lingual lesson. After the student has mastered and memorized the dialogue through classroom and laboratory practice, he is ready to see the written text for his first association with the written symbolization of what he has learned. This order of procedure is dictated by the desire to avoid interference from written symbols until after the student has acquired the foundation of good audio-lingual habits.

Hayes discusses the nature of interference from the native language in the *Teacher's Manual* accompanying *A-LM Spanish, Level I*.[2] To understand these interferences it is necessary to understand the relationship which the educated native speaker of English perceives between the sounds of language and the graphic symbols used to represent them on paper. There is a constant interplay between words and sentences as heard and words and sentences as printed. What he hears said and what he sees written have become the same thing for him, resulting from a long training process during which he built up a whole system of automatic responses to letters and words on the printed page. These responses are so deeply ingrained that they become to him the only possible responses. As Hayes points out, the secondary-school student has been exposed to such training for a shorter time than has the "educated native," but as he seeks to acquire the different habits of a new language, it should be no surprise that native language habits frequently interpose themselves.

Just as speaking is hindered by the tendency to produce native sounds rather than foreign ones and to form sentences according to native rather than foreign models, so, too, when written symbols are introduced, a powerful interference is at hand. Students of Spanish are already familiar with the Roman alphabet and have established relationships between these symbols and English sounds, words, and sentences. It is now their task to learn to associate Spanish sounds, still relatively new to them, with these same alphabet symbols, and the tendency will be strong to let English responses prevail.

Unless the teacher is vigilant, the new habits of speech carefully acquired early in the audio-lingual course will be noticeably set back when the written symbol is introduced. It is not only the established

---

[2] *Teacher's Manual, Spanish, Level I* (New York: Harcourt, Brace & World, 1964).

association of sounds and single letters which interferes but also groups of letters, whole words, and even sentences. Obvious examples are those printed words which contain combinations of letters which could occur easily in English or in Spanish: *general, canal, probable,* etc.

The *A-LM Teacher's Manual* (p. 56) offers the following suggestions to minimize interference when the written symbol is introduced:

1. Explain briefly to the class the nature of the problem. Caution them to be on guard at all times against the tendency to respond in a typically English fashion. Instill in them a pride in keeping their hard-won Spanish speaking habits intact.
2. Insist on the same high standards of pronunciation that prevailed throughout the course.
3. When you name sounds or letters, be very sure to make clear which of these you are talking about. *Sounds are what is heard; letters are marks on paper.* Form the habit of saying that a given sound is *represented* in a certain way, that a given letter or sequence of letters *represents* a certain sound.
4. Always use the Spanish names of the letters of the alphabet.

"Reading" implies two meanings: (1) to pronounce words and sentences aloud in response to a stimulus of a printed word, and (2) to follow printed or written sequences rapidly for comprehension, with the eye scanning whole groups of words or sentences at a time. It is clear that the student must control the sound-letter correspondences of the new language if he is to acquire the first basic skill mentioned above. It is equally clear that other techniques will be required to lay the foundation for the long-range reading skill: rapid reading for comprehension. Extensive practice is required for both, and specific drills have been devised:

1. *Mass association practice.* This requires reading aloud material already mastered audio-lingually.
2. *Interference drill.* This drill elicits an oral response to Spanish letters or letter sequences which signal something quite different to the native speaker of English, such as *h, j, z, r, v.*
3. *Graphic minimal pairs.* The difference to the eye between *gue* and *güe,* for example, is two dots. The student accustomed to reading English does not readily attach significance to this written distinction. By pairing words containing *gu* with words containing *gü* and eliciting an oral response, the visual cue is emphasized.
4. *Graphic representation of difficult sound contrasts.* Partially overlapping with the third type of reading drill, this drill elicits oral

responses to the paired graphic representations of difficult sound contrasts in Spanish, such as *d/r*, or *e/ei*. It is to be expected that the student will still have pronunciation difficulties here, and special drill on the written differences should help to focus the student's attention on the corresponding difference in sound.

But let us return to the use of the dialogue of the audio-lingual lesson for intensive reading. As was said before, the students are ready to see the written text *after* they have mastered the dialogue orally. They are then led to repeat the dialogue several times with the written text before them, associating the oral with the written form. During this process, known as "mass association practice," the teacher must take care not to analyze the written form in any way. Some methodologists suggest a third step, which is to have the pupils repeat the dialogues silently to themselves several times as a reinforcement. Others, perhaps more wisely, suggest that reinforcement be accomplished by repeating aloud after the stimulus of the laboratory tape and with the written text of the dialogue visible.

The next stage in intensive reading corresponds to the longer stretches of prose which are generally added fairly early in the first year (cf. samples of early reading selections in *Modern Spanish*, second edition, p. 73, and in *A-LM, Level I*, p. 122). The recommended procedure for presenting these readings is first, for the teacher (or tape) to read the selection, while pupils listen but do not look at any printed material. In the second step, the teacher (or tape) reads again, while the students follow the printed text silently. The third step is a rereading by the teacher in short phrases with appropriate pauses, so that the students can repeat in chorus the phrase just heard. It is often recommended that at the conclusion of the repetition of a group of sentences or a paragraph, the teacher ask short and simple questions eliciting short answers from the students. These short answers are then expanded by the teacher to form complete utterances which are modelled and echoed by the class as a reinforcement of the original choral repetitions. Fourth, the teacher and students read together the entire selection chorally without pauses, approximating normal speed. As pupils demonstrate proficiency, and as time permits, either in the classroom or in the laboratory, they may read aloud individually for reinforcement.

After the fourth or fifth reading done as suggested above, the procedures for intensive reading are gradually changed. Oral presentation by teacher or tape will decrease gradually. Eventually, the teacher or tape will read the selection to the students only once and choral repetitions will be limited to certain more difficult sections of the selection.

A new set of problems arises, however, which must be met by antici-
pation drills. When readings from sources other than the initial audio-
lingual text are introduced in the third and fourth semesters, pupils
will encounter more and more material which they have not directly
experienced audio-lingually; steps must, therefore, be taken to anticipate
any special difficulties. Generally, this takes the form of noting the new
material and drilling it intensively as above. The more the reading
program progresses, the more new material is going to be met and the
more necessary becomes this type of anticipatory drilling.

One technical point remains for us in our discussion of the intensive
reading phase: testing. In many audio-lingual texts, a set of questions
accompanies the intensive reading selections (cf. *A-LM, Level I*, p. 156)
which serves as an adequate checkup. Where such questionnaires are
not available, the teacher should prepare something of the sort — in
the form of multiple-choice questions or sentences to be completed with
the newly introduced words and phrases — comprehensive enough to
test the students' understanding. Question-and-answer practice after
each selection helps fix the content in the pupils' minds and crystallize
salient points of the story as it progresses, if it is continued over several
units. True-false statements or direct-content questions are also useful.
But it must be remembered that true-false statements are statistically
inadequate for most testing purposes.

The third year, especially as it leads into the fourth, sees the intensive
reading program diminish in favor of extensive reading. In this period,
intensive reading will be more and more limited to passages selected
for special interest or for the importance of the structural elements they
present, and oral reading will be dropped. Silent reading is, after all,
the most useful form for the pupil, and it is in the third year that it
becomes a major goal. The emphasis now shifts to the rapid, extensive
reading of a wide range of material containing elements for enriching
the students' knowledge of culture and literature. This is the stage
which Fries has called that of "vivid imaginative realization." It is the
stage in which the reading process becomes so automatic that the reader
uses reading as fully as the spoken language in acquiring and assimilat-
ing new experiences. Reading of this kind also fulfills the "literary
purpose," where language is used not simply to communicate facts and
information but to provide vivid imaginative realizations of actions,
emotions, and values.

The ability to respond to artistic materials of literature presented in
Spanish is achieved only by constant practice; by learning the linguistic
material included in the "code" of literature; by learning to identify
particular meanings in particular situations; by discussing the cultural

implications in the use of the language; by analyzing, in a gradually more complex fashion, the style of the author, the characters of the literary personalities; by discussing in Spanish the cultural content, the plot, etc. Periodicals and newspapers should also be included. The very nature of the skill being acquired implies independence, but the teacher must take care to provide selections within the pupils' linguistic powers and should continue to train them in rapid reading for comprehension.

The best audio-lingual materials provide reading selections as a part of each lesson, so that the student is ready to proceed to the reading of edited texts as a next step. Assuming that language instruction is begun in the seventh grade, with audio-lingual materials, the transition from intensive reading to extensive silent reading should be accomplished during the second semester of the eighth grade. By the ninth grade, the pupil is generally ready to begin the extensive reading program. Here, the junior high school teacher has a greater problem than has his high school counterpart, for junior high school readings must take into account the different psychology of the pupil. In this sense, reading selections should be of a length to be completed in a reasonably short time. Reading content should include approximately equal doses of cultural information and literary content. The choice of appropriate literary material is, therefore, a vital one.

The oral approach has shown plays to be the most satisfactory first extensive readings, since these adapt themselves equally well to silent or oral reading. Students should demonstrate proficiency with plays, before being advanced to novels (perhaps with short stories in between). Poetry may be used at all levels, provided it is straightforward and easily understood, given in small doses. Poems give a good opportunity for oral reading and, if short enough, can easily be memorized. Such memorization is enjoyed by many pupils and gives them a sense of satisfaction and achievement. Periodicals can also be used toward the end of the ninth grade, but the special nature of "journalese" makes even simple articles difficult to read.

There should be a small reference collection, including dictionaries and a reference grammar, in the classroom. Students should be encouraged to acquire a dictionary for their own use but need to be carefully instructed in how to use it. The more compendious ones often give too little information, and the more comprehensive ones often give more than the student will know how to use unless he is guided.

In the three-year high school, the above comments apply to the eleventh grade, where first instruction was begun in the tenth grade. The twelfth-grade program in such schools puts the emphasis on literary works and periodicals. A good supply of Spanish-language newspapers and magazines should be available in the classroom. (Some of the more easily acquired might include: *El mundo hispánico, Visión,* and *Hoy,* for magazines, and the newspapers *Excelsior* from Mexico City, *ABC* from Madrid, and *La Nación* from Buenos Aires.) [3] Literary works should be selected from recent Spanish-American and Spanish writing in competent editions. As students progress, the works should become steadily more difficult. They may be correlated for topics for oral reports, etc. In systems in which a six-year sequence, from grade 7 to grade 12, is maintained, the eleventh and twelfth years call for extensive reading of literary and cultural works, with attention to literary style, the author's biography and his place in literature, the technique of the work, the author's purpose, and his philosophy. "Classics," in the sense of works from centuries earlier than our own, are not necessarily wise choices for the reading program even at the eleventh- and twelfth-grade levels. Often they involve stylistic and cultural problems which call for considerable literary and historical sophistication on the part of the students. More recent writing of unquestionable literary value may serve better the purpose of leading the student more widely and deeply into the language and culture without forcing him to leap great barriers of style and concept.

Writing is the fourth of the skills presented in the fundamental skills approach and is the last to be introduced. For this reason, the writing skill is based primarily on what pupils can say and partly on what they can read. From the practical viewpoint of using the language, writing is probably the skill for which students will find the least demand. Still, it is important in reinforcing what has been learned audio-lingually and also in giving the pupils a chance for self-expression. Some linguists have also suggested that pupils learn to observe the intricacies and the overall structure of the language most accurately through composition. Of course, the goal of writing in the fundamental skills approach is free and creative composition, expressing the pupil's individuality. The goal is reached, however, through a process of writing practice which is both guided and imitative.

Generally, imitative writing is introduced shortly after reading. The first step is for the pupil to write the very same material that he mastered during his audio-lingual practice. Practice in the exact writing of a few authentic phrases is most helpful. Thus, he continues the use of mean-

---

[3] For information on sources of subscriptions to Spanish-language periodicals, see Esther Eaton and Mary Hayes, *Source Materials for Secondary School Teachers of Foreign Languages* (Washington, D.C.: USOE. Bulletin OE–27001–C; circular 768, 1966), 10–11.

ingful word groups and avoids recourse to English. This work can be accomplished outside of class.

The second type of imitative writing exercise which is normally used is dictation. Its value lies in the many aspects of language learning involved in its performance. The student must listen intently so as to differentiate sounds and distinguish words and breath groups. He must, of course, understand meaning, and this involves the recognition of form and structure. Furthermore, he must understand the spelling system, including the use of diacritical marks and the use of capitals and punctuation marks. The teacher, in preparing and reading the dictation, should be careful to base the exercise upon material which the student has already heard and seen. One must remember that short dictations done at frequent intervals have been shown to give better results than lengthy ones at longer intervals. The following is a procedure recommended for administering dictation:

Dictation Procedure

I. Preliminaries
   A. Tell students exactly how you will proceed.
   B. Make sure students are acquainted thoroughly with the terminology of punctuation in the target language.
   C. Be sure that the material for dictation is of reasonable length (teachers have used as few as 25 or as many as 100 words successfully).
   D. Be sure that the material for dictation is already familiar or easily induced from aural-oral experience.

II. Dictation
   A. Read selection at normal ("broadcast") speed.
   B. Read selection again, pausing at each breath group [4] (5-cycle format with choral repetition).
   C. Read selection again at normal speed.

---

[4] A breath group is the amount of speech normally and comfortably uttered on a single expulsion of air from the lungs. A breath group need not correspond to any particular length of utterance and does not end except where a pause is considered possible in the language. Thus, English speakers would not normally pause between the *good* and *morning* of *good morning;* therefore, it would be uttered as a single breath group. They might also utter the longer sentence 'what he got and what he wanted were two different things' in one breath group, but would more likely subdivide it into two or even three breath groups: 'what he got and what he wanted/ are two different things,' or 'what he got/ and what he wanted/ are two different things.' The latter is characteristic of slower, more deliberate speech and is, consequently, the type of grouping we would expect in a dictation.

D. Read selection in breath groups; students write in each pause.
E. Read selection at normal speed; students check what they have written.

Immediate correction is vital in all dictation. Perhaps the best means of providing this immediate correction, while still permitting the teacher to collect the student's written work is the following: each student is provided with two sheets of paper stapled together with a piece of carbon paper in between. The first page is blank. The upper half of the second page is blank, but the lower half contains the correct version of the dictation. The students write the dictation on the upper half of the first page, tear it off, and hand it in. The second page then permits an immediate comparison between what they wrote and the correct version.

As the pupils demonstrate proficiency in handling the dictation exercise, a further step can be taken, which is still a form of writing from aural comprehension. There are several possibilities which can be used in any order or mixed together as the pupil's progress permits. First, a passage is read twice at normal speed. It is a passage selected, like the dictations, from material with which the pupils are already familiar, aurally and visually. Several short questions on the material are asked orally, each question repeated twice. The passage and questions are then read a third time for double-checking. As a variation, the teacher makes incomplete statements about the selection read instead of asking questions about it. Pupils are required to complete the statement in Spanish. For more sophisticated groups, instead of questions or incomplete statements, students are required to restate the passage, either in their own words or in another person or tense. It must be remembered throughout that the real meaning of diacritic markings and punctuation will become clearer through this phase of instruction.

When students are able to perform adequately in the foregoing exercises, the transition to free composition can be initiated through a "guided" composition phase. The first step is for students to write exercises involving drill patterns reviewed in class. Thus, after doing, say "Paso 7" of Michalski, *Spanish: Oral Approach I*, or "Lección novena" in Staubach, Eldon, Walsh, *Second Year Spanish*, revised edition, the substitution drills on pages 113 and 181 respectively may be duplicated and given to the student for written drill. Patterned response drills (such as in Hansen and Wilkins *Español a lo vivo*, p. 82) form the basis for another variation, in which students write answers to a series of carefully formulated questions (already familiar to them audio-lingually) which contain speech patterns that provide a basis for the answers.

Pupils progress from this "guided" writing stage to a "controlled" writing stage. Here, pupils change passages from one tense or person to another, change dialogue to narrative or the reverse, summarize passages, etc., with the teacher gradually lessening the controls. Students are also required to formulate a connected passage to dramatize or describe a situation which the teacher suggests. Gradually, students may be allowed to progress to full freedom in writing original and individual compositions. In all cases, the linguistic content will have been familiar to the student, both audio-lingually and visually, prior to the time of the writing exercise, thus preserving the prescribed order of hearing, speaking, reading, and writing.

It is impossible to lay down positive rules for correlating the successive periods of writing with particular courses and levels; too much depends upon the success of the course and the achievement of the students. Writing is, perhaps, that phase of the fundamental skills approach which most depends upon the progress of the individual pupil. Thus, any indication of grade or level can be only approximate. Generally, the phase of writing from aural comprehension lasts for roughly the first year. The second year is devoted to guided writing, an occasional exercise in writing from aural comprehension, ending with, perhaps, some controlled writing. Controlled writing, leading to controlled composition, is the chief concern of the writing portion of the third year program. Free composition, to be truly profitable, requires a linguistic sophistication found for the most part only in advanced students, i.e., those of the fourth year.

Prospective reading texts for the foreign language class should be subjected to the same rigorous scrutiny and evaluation as the basic language textbook itself. The following checklist provides some of the more essential criteria for such evaluation. The categories reflect the major considerations taken up in this chapter and relevant issues discussed in Chapter 12.

  (a) authenticity of language
  (b) authenticity of cultural image
  (c) vocabulary of high frequency
  (d) controlled density of new vocabulary
  (e) controlled density of new sentence types
  (f) spacing and reintroduction of new vocabulary and sentence types
  (g) "preview" of especially difficult new vocabulary and sentence types via basic sentences or similar devices.
  (h) "what to look for" guide with reference to content

READING AND WRITING IN THE AUDIO-LINGUAL APPROACH

(i) follow-up exercise material:
 1. vocabulary (by inference, not by translation)
 2. content
 3. structures (by pattern drill)
(j) correlated audio or visual program (or both)
(k) monolingual glossary or notes [5]

▶ EXERCISES

1. Discuss the function of *supplementary reading* in the fundamental skills approach.
2. Contrast *intensive* and *extensive* reading, and specify their respective uses in the fundamental skills approach.
3. Discuss the principal aims of the writing program in the fundamental skills approach.
4. What preliminary steps should be taken before the pupil is permitted to write a free composition? Describe how each step fulfills a basic need in the development of the pupil's skills to prepare him for free composition.
5. Discuss the point at which reading and writing become a part of the audio-lingual program.
6. Show how reading selections can be presented to the student audio-lingually.
7. To what extent is it important that a reading selection reflect contrastive aspects of the culture of which the target language is an expression?
8. How long do edited texts have to be continued before it is possible to use material that has not been edited or adapted at all?
9. What remedial steps can be used to cope with frequently recurring errors in written composition?

REFERENCE BOOKS AND ARTICLES

Broz, James and Alfred Hayes, eds. *Linguistics and Reading* (Washington, D.C.: Center for Applied Linguistics, 1966).

Carroll, John. "The Analysis of Reading Instruction" (*Yearbook of the National Society for the Study of Education*, 1964).

Edfeldt, Ake W. *Silent Speech and Silent Reading* (Chicago: University of Chicago Press, 1960).

Fries, Charles C. *Linguistics and Reading* (New York: Holt, Rinehart and Winston, 1963).

---

[5] For how monolingual notes and glossaries are constructed, see David M. Feldman and Gerald L. Boarino, *Lecturas contemporáneas* (Waltham, Mass.: Blaisdell, 1967).

GRAY, WILLIAM S. *The Teaching of Reading and Writing* (Paris: UNESCO, 1956).

LEFEVRE, CARL A. *Linguistics and the Teaching of Reading* (New York: McGraw-Hill, 1964).

PROCHOROFF, MARINA *et al.* "Writing as Expression," in *Reports of the Working Committees of the 1963 Northeast Conference on the Teaching of Foreign Languages.*

SCHERER, GEORGE A. C. *A System for Teaching Modern Foreign Language Reading,* "Teacher's Notebook" Series (New York: Harcourt, Brace and World, 1964).

——, *et al.* "Reading for Meaning," in *Reports of the Working Committees of the 1963 Northeast Conference on the Teaching of Foreign Languages.*

SCOTT, CHARLES. "The Linguistic Basis for the Development of the Reading Skill" (*Modern Language Journal* 50, 1966), 535–544.

WEST, MICHAEL P. *The Construction of Reading Material for Teaching a Foreign Language* (London: Oxford University Press, 1927).

8

Testing and evaluation

Testing in the foreign language program can be divided into three distinct categories:

1. Aptitude testing — designed to help group students in multiple-track programs and, in some cases, when correlated with classroom performance over a one- or two-year period, to assist in counselling students who are experiencing difficulties;
2. Proficiency testing — designed to evaluate cognitive and skill gains in one or more language skills;
3. Diagnostic testing — designed to reveal strengths and weaknesses in students' control of the language so that adjustment in the teaching program may be made to increase or decrease the amount of emphasis on given sounds or structures, as the case may be.

The second of these testing modalities is by far the most frequently used in the foreign language program. Its aim is to permit the teacher to judge pupils' ability, progress, and achievement by frequent, systematic, and purposeful tests. Although this definition bears a close resemblance to the principles of an effective testing program as developed in other fields, evaluation of progress in a foreign language involves special considerations which we shall discuss here. It has often been said that, because each drill in the audio-lingual lesson presupposes that the student have mastered preceding material, no testing program is needed beyond the correct daily performance of the drills and exercises. While this is partly true, it fails to recognize the importance of testing for other than immediate achievement. Long-range achievement, deficiencies, placement, and diagnosis of the program itself are all factors which must be measured by group and individual testing of a nature more comprehensive than that of the single audio-lingual structural drill.

Thus, the overall theory of testing in the fundamental skills approach is not only to measure the skills and knowledge taught but also to motivate the student to better learning and to point up weak spots in the program itself. The test results provide the teacher with a basis for generalization and comparison necessary for the measurement of progress.

Throughout our discussion, we have said that the audio-lingual course is divided into four separate units: listening, speaking, reading, and writing. Although we now know that all of these skills are tied closely together in the program itself and frequently overlap, it is often convenient to divide them and deal with them separately in methodological discussion, as we have been doing. In testing, likewise, all four skills should be tested, both collectively and individually. Collective measurement gives us a practical index of achievement for communication goals so long as that complex of skills required on the examination is natural in normal language behavior.

Among other ground rules of language testing, our examination of the fundamental skills approach leads us to conclude that the question-answer technique in the foreign language is useful for testing speaking and listening skills, in addition to its common use for testing the manipulation of structure. But we must remember that the spoken answer to an aurally perceived question or the written answer to a visually perceived question automatically involves the simultaneous correct functioning of their separate skills: hearing and speaking, and reading and writing, respectively. In measuring skills individually, questions must be designed to eliminate as much as possible the use of other skills. The skills tested should be based upon those taught in class as part of normal language behavior in the area tested. Thus, idioms, vocabulary, and structures should be tested in context in active uses. Cultural items should be tested in a situationally and linguistically authentic context.

Many teachers prefer to avoid using incorrect forms on a test in the belief that the correcting of incorrect forms is a test type best reserved for students who have already mastered the language and are learning to teach it. If the correction were the *only* purpose in presenting incorrect items on a test, these objections would be valid. However, where a test item involves the pupil's selecting a "best" form out of several possible forms, some of which might be incorrect, there is less objection. The decisive factor in exercising this judgment is in the definition of the term "incorrect." If by "incorrect" we mean a misspelled or structurally impossible, or erroneous form, then the injunction against their use is valid, for we risk focusing the student's attention on faulty usage. If it is a matter of *appropriate* forms, all of which are possible but only one likely to be used in this context by educated natives, then the inclusion of the less appropriate form is valid, since the exercise serves to test the pupil's "feeling" for the language.[1] The teacher must be careful, however, always to warn the pupils in advance when to expect items on an examination that may be incorrect in this sense.

Translation is a tricky matter in testing. Translation from target to source language has no place except on the most advanced types of tests where the focus is on the pupil's ability to render accurately into English material of a specialized nature, such as technical articles, foreign correspondence, or directions; or material of a literary nature which he must render into comparable English style. Clearly, these are not the goals of the high school language program. Nor are translations from English into the target language recommended as a testing device. However, in the best audio-lingual texts, translation drills have been judiciously employed to point out the differences of structure between the target and the source languages. Such drills may serve for purposes of testing (Cf. pp. 78–79). Their use is, at best, limited to situations in which only the direct comparison of the English form with the target language will elicit the correct answers or will determine, in limited circumstances, whether or not the student has succeeded in putting aside the influence of his native language structure, for example: "He isn't a loyal *friend*" as opposed to "He isn't a *loyal* friend" to get the answers, "*No es un leal amigo*" as opposed to "*No es un amigo leal*" (from *Modern Spanish*, second edition, pp. 192–193), or the contrast between "like" and *gustar*.

Within these general limits, the preparation of the tests themselves can begin. Instructions to the student should be made clear and succinct. Directions may be given in the foreign language, although this is not totally necessary. When the directions cannot easily be understood by the students, they should be given in English. Where necessary, a model of the item and its target might be supplied. It is frequently helpful to read test instructions aloud with the students before the test itself begins. Test results are frequently invalidated when students who know the material are delayed or confused by complicated instructions.

The sampling of items should be representative. The audio-lingual

---

[1] Cf. "Rejoinders in the Listening Comprehension Tests" in *A-LM* Teacher's Manuals.

pattern drills themselves often serve as good test focuses for specific structural points. In the larger tests, it is wise to select from a broad stock of structural items. This is not to deny, however, that the relative weights of questions should be distributed in proportion to the importance of the skill or knowledge measured. Economy is achieved in selecting test items by choosing those which represent the most efficient evaluation per unit of pupil time spent. The complaint about unfair testing is often motivated by a failure to match the testing emphases with the major language learning activities in the classroom. If, let us say, we are in the phase of instruction in which a majority of the time is spent on oral drill, dialogue memorization and adaptation, and the like, then the aural and oral skills are those which should figure most prominently in the tests.

Pupils should always have experience with question types before being tested. If a test question type is to be used which the students do not know from their daily class work, practice should be conducted in class prior to the test, to acquaint them with the operation.

In the discussion that follows, we shall consider seven skills which are commonly tested as a part of the audio-lingual program.

I. *Testing listening skills.* In testing listening skills it is imperative that the teacher clearly distinguish, in the preparation of the test, between the testing of the sound patterns of the language and the testing of meanings associated with the sounds. While these two aspects will be fused into one skill as the learner advances, it is best that they be treated separately at the beginning levels, since the effective comprehension of meanings is dependent upon a thorough training in the recognition of contrastive sounds.

A. *Recognition of sounds.* The general technique in the testing of this skill is simple: the teacher (or tape) reads aloud one or more utterances and the students, who may respond in a variety of ways, are then checked to see if they have recognized the problem sound or contrast. This type of test is ideal for the language laboratory where the high fidelity of reproduction and the comparative isolation of the student in his booth are aids to better performance. There are a number of ways to accomplish this, some of which are discussed by Lado in *Language Testing.*[2]

---

[2] Robert Lado, *Language Testing* (New York: McGraw-Hill, 1965), pp. 46–53; 123–133.

One of these is the sound-to-sound method, in which the student is asked to compare one sound with another and to indicate if they are the same or different. A method commonly used is that in which the teacher reads minimal pairs (e.g., *peso/paso, pero/perro*), and the student indicates *S* for "same" and *D* for "different" on an answer sheet. Another is that in which the teacher reads groups of three or four words and the students indicate (by writing 1, 2, 3, or 4) which ones have the same initial phoneme; e.g., (1) *peso* (2) *paso* (3) *besa* (4) *pozo*. It is also possible to ask the student to indicate that he perceives the difference between a sound in the target language and a similar sound in the source language (e.g., English *low* as against Spanish *lo*). For this exercise, preprinted answer sheets containing columns of letters or numbers may be provided.

Often the student is provided with an answer sheet which has the words listed under each item and he is to mark the written word or phrase that matches what the model will say. For example, the stimulus *lee* is given by the model, with the following written choices on the student's paper: *lee, leí, ley, lea*. As we have said elsewhere, however, this technique is questionable in the early stages of language learning, since the student is being asked to make the transition from sound to graphic symbol, thereby involving, in a small but meaningful way, the additional skills of reading and/or writing.

Intonation patterns can also be tested in the ways suggested above. Here the student is asked to distinguish between contrastive patterns within the language. For example, he is to indicate (by writing 1, 2, or 3 on his paper) which of the following utterances is a question:

(1) "¿Van al centro hoy?"   (2) "Van al centro hoy."

(3) "¡Van al centro hoy!"

Or the student may be asked to distinguish which of the following utterances indicates that the sentence is not complete:

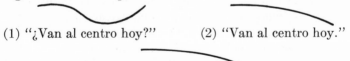

(1) "Pablo viene a casa."   (2) "Pablo viene a casa. . . ."

(3) "Pablo, ¿viene a casa?"

B. *Recognition of meanings.* It is important to mention again that testing for listening comprehension at the beginning levels must not depend on the co-functioning of another skill. The student must not be expected to produce an oral response to an item on a comprehension test, for he is then faced with the double task of *understanding* the item and *producing* a response; he may, in his nervousness, be unable to respond well, orally or in writing, even though he has understood the stimulus perfectly. In other words, testing for *comprehension* is not testing for *production* of the language. (This criterion invalidates such tests as those in which the teacher reads a series of questions which the students are to take down as a dictation, then instructs the students to write answers to these questions. The resulting confusion frequently means that the student is doubly penalized, for if he cannot accurately associate graphic symbols with the sounds of the stimulus, then it is impossible to write a correct response.)

Some of the more common ways of testing recognition are:

(1) True-false test. The teacher reads a number of true-false statements based on a passage which the students have heard twice. The students respond by circling *Sí* or *No*, which are provided on the answer sheets. A variation of this test is one in which the statement is not based on any particular narrative, but merely general information (based on specific vocabulary), such as "El árbol tiene dos ojos," "Hay helado de postre," "El perro vive en el agua," etc., the first and third eliciting the *No* response, the second eliciting *Sí*.

(2) Multiple-choice tests: Rejoinders. Tests involving suitable rejoinders are familiar to most teachers. The teacher reads a statement twice (*not always a question*); three or four possible replies or rejoinders are read and the student indicates (by circling A, B, C, D, on his answer sheet) which is most suitable. For example:

¡Qué frío hace!
   (A) **Sí, menos mal que hace calor.**
   (B) **Bueno, vamos a clase.**
   (C) **Justamente por eso no quiero salir.**
   (D) **No sé. ¿Qué hace Vd.?**

(3) Multiple-choice tests: Completion. A statement is read, which is not complete, with the teacher indicating by some

gesture where the "blank" in the statement is. Three or four possible short completions are then read and the student indicates his choice. For example:

Yo soy hijo único. No tengo _____
  (A) **primos**
  (B) **hijos**
  (C) **años**
  (D) **hermanos**

In composing the last two types of tests, care must be taken not to make the alternatives structurally impossible or ridiculous in meaning so that the student is able to isolate the correct completion exclusively by a process of elimination.

After the reading and writing skills have become a more significant part of the course, these same multiple-choice tests may be used to measure aural comprehension through visual recognition of the correct answer to an oral stimulus. In this case the student is provided with an answer sheet containing the four alternatives for each item. He hears the stimulus, then marks on his sheet the rejoinder or completion of his choice.

(4) Student performs in response to a cue. When the student's vocabulary is adequate to permit a variety of command cues, a test may be composed in which he is given a series of rapid-fire instructions to which he must react on his paper. For example, he has before him a drawing of several animals and is instructed to circle the dog; or he is asked to draw a house containing six rooms and a staircase.

II. *Testing speaking skill: production tests.* As we mentioned in our discussion of the language laboratory, more experimenting has been done with the problems encountered in the speaking tests than with any other. This has led to the establishment of a fairly uniform set of goals in giving speaking tests. First, we test the pupils' ability to reproduce the individual allophones of the foreign language, as well as longer sequences and relevant intonation patterns. Second, we test their ability to express their thoughts in the foreign language, in response either to a question or to some other stimulus. Third, we test their oral control of one or several of the structural patterns or of the vocabulary of the foreign language through appropriate questions or pattern drills. Although the teacher may choose to test for one or another aspect of the speaking skill, it is also possible to combine all three.

The simplest of all speaking tests is the echo test. The pupil simply repeats as accurately as he can whatever the teacher (or tape) says. A variation on this is the "buildup" echo test, in which pupils repeat sentences whose length is progressively increased. Such tests are difficult to score. The teacher should prepare in advance a checklist of the specific phonological problems he wishes to measure, limiting the number of different items to be measured on a given test. The teacher then gives a rating for each focus. This type of scoring has two major advantages: it may be used just as easily for other types of speaking tests to measure sound production, and it also allows the teacher to keep a cumulative chart for each pupil to measure his achievement and progress in phonological reproduction. A sample of this type of scoring sheet is given at the end of this chapter.

As the course progresses, more variations of testing become suitable. Some of the types used for testing comprehension may now be adapted, such as that involving completion (i.e., "En casa desayunamos _____." The student may, of course, respond in several ways: "a las siete," "en el comedor," "muy poco," etc.). The free-rejoinder type may be used to give the student some choice within the limits of his ability. For example, to the cue: "Enrique está en el hospital," the student could reply correctly: "¡Qué lástima!", "¿Qué le ha pasado?", "Sí, tiene una pierna quebrada," etc.

No mention need be made of the validity of the traditional question-and-answer type test here. A variation of this, however, somewhat more difficult, is that test in which the student is given a statement and instructed to phrase a question for which that statement is a possible answer.

Other techniques of testing speaking production are: student discussion of a picture; retelling a narrative which he has just heard; summarizing a story he has read; composing a dialogue about a situation, or a picture, presented to him; and the directed dialogue.

III. *Testing grammatical structure.* The testing criterion here is the student's ability to formulate a specific pattern in situational contexts. The older test types in which we focused our attention on translation from one language to the other, or in which we required forms to be identified with regard to grammatical nomenclature, do not perform this function and are, consequently, no longer useful to us.

Many of the standard audio-lingual drill forms may be used as test items, thus minimizing our dependence upon special "test" types. Some pattern drill types actually began as test types, especially the integration (combination) forms. (Cf. also Chapter 5.) In these the students are required to combine two utterances in order to test their ability to use certain structures, such as relative forms and adverbial phrases. Thus to the cue "María es bonita. Luisa es bonita también," the student responds with the combined form: "Luisa es tan bonita como María." Similarly, "Acá viene nuestro amigo. El trae los libros" is combined into: "Acá viene nuestro amigo que trae los libros," and if the student is instructed to use al-plus-infinitive, he will combine "Escribió la lección. Se le acabó la tinta." into "Al escribir la lección se le acabó la tinta."

The directed dialogue type of drill can also be useful in testing grammatical structure. For example, in testing command forms, the cue "Dígale a Juan que debe venir pronto" will elicit the response: "Juan, ¡ven pronto!" To the statement: "Pregúntele a Luisa si le gusta cantar" the student will reply: "Luisa, ¿te gusta cantar?", etc.

Lado discusses the use of pictures with specific content and instructions which predetermine the structure to be used and tested.[3] For example, a series of pictures could present a girl eating various things, playing with her dog, talking with her teacher, etc. Some of the possible instructions which could elicit responses with specific structural items are: a) "Tell me what you see" (to test complete sentences in the present tense); b) "This happened yesterday. Tell me what happened" (for the use of the past tenses); c) "This was happening yesterday. Tell me what was happening" (to test use of the progressive forms); d) "What happened to the girl?" (for the use of the passive voice, i.e., "She was bitten by the dog.").

Responses of could, would, might could be tested with a more complex picture showing a fence and a tree, with a cat on one side of the fence, a rat on the other. The instruction is: "Describe all the possibilities for the rat if the cat were to jump over the fence." Possible responses would include remarks such as: "If the cat jumped over the fence, he would eat the rat; . . ., the rat

---

[3] *Language Testing*, pp. 171–175.

would climb the tree; . . ., the rat would run around the fence," etc.

A picture might contain several images in a situation and the student is instructed to reproduce the conversation which presumably takes place.

With a bit of imagination and possibly the help of the art teacher, the Spanish teacher can develop a series of pictures which may be used for several years for a variety of purposes, since the same picture will often serve to test various structures, vocabulary, etc., at different times in the testing program.

IV. *Testing vocabulary and idioms.* Testing for mastery of vocabulary and idiomatic expressions may be accomplished either actively or passively. It is imperative that the use of English always be avoided in testing vocabulary. The many possibilities provided by the use of pictures have been discussed or implied above. In addition to asking questions about the pictures, the teacher may utilize fully the question-answer type pertaining to general situations or information involving the vocabulary under study, or he may vary the format by constructing completion-type items, such as "El opuesto de bueno es _____." Variety may be added by the teacher's giving a definition and asking the student to give the word being defined, i.e., "¿Cómo se llama el hombre que cocina el pan?" (*el panadero*). In more advanced sections, the above procedure may be reversed; that is, the teacher gives the word *panadero* and elicits a short definition from the student.

The most widely used forms for passive testing of vocabulary are:

I. *Associating ideas in one column with ideas in another:*

1. Completion

A	*B*
Llevo guantes en	( ) **los pies**
	( ) **la cabeza**
	( ) **las manos**
	( ) **los hombros**

2. Matching

a)

A	*B*
En seguida	( ) **Ahora mismo**
	( ) **De repente**
	( ) **Otra vez**
	( ) **De vez en cuando**

b) (A passive variant of the active definition test suggested above)

A	B
_____ **El primer mes del año**	1. **tío**
_____ **El hombre que cocina pan**	2. **presidente**
_____ **El hermano de mi padre**	3. **enero**
etc.	4. **panadero**
	5. **diciembre**
	6. **zapatero**

(It is always important in this type of matching test that more items be given in Column B than are necessary to complete the set in Column A, thus avoiding the students' responding by the process of elimination.)

II. *Associating synonyms and antonyms:*

A	B
trabajador	( ) **perezoso**
	( ) **aplicado**
	( ) **bonachón**
	( ) **tacaño**

V. *Testing reading.* As we have seen, reading plays a part in other tests already mentioned, since by definition, it is a skill which requires that the student have a knowledge of both vocabulary and structure. Consequently, many of the testing types suggested here for testing reading proficiency will have a similarity to types already mentioned in preceding sections.

In the early stages, at least, it is essential that the teacher measure the learner's reading skill independently of his ability in the other skills. Some of the most widely-used devices for this purpose are:

1. *True-False Items.* Students are asked to read a series of printed statements and to indicate whether they are true (T) or false (F). These may be based on some passage studied previously, or they may be random statements utilizing familiar vocabulary:

> Los peces viven en el agua. (T)
> El sol se pone en el este. (F)

A variation of the above test is one in which the student is provided with a picture and a series of true or false statements regarding the picture. The student is then asked to indicate his decision with T or F.

2. *Multiple-Choice Items.* Two other popular types are those resembling the "rejoinder" test used in testing listening comprehension. a) The student reads a key statement and must then choose the most logical accompanying statement from a list provided:

1) Gustavo está muy cansado.

   A) Le falta dinero.
   B) Ha trabajado mucho.
   C) Su hermana lo acompañó a la fiesta.

2) ¡Qué día más bonito!

   A) Me siento mal.
   B) Vamos a la playa.
   C) Espérame en la puerta.

b) *Question-and-answer type,* in which students select the most logical answer to a question:

¿Quieres ir al cine esta noche?

   A) Sí, gracias, tengo ganas de dormir.
   B) Gracias, no, tengo que trabajar en casa.
   C) No, está descompuesto mi tocadiscos.

The reader will notice that the only difference between these items and others discussed elsewhere as learning devices and testing types is in the manner of presentation. Here there is no testing of the listening skill, since all the materials are presented in written form.

3. *Passage Items.* The student is given a printed passage to read. A wide range of test types may then follow, but care must be taken in all of them that the test questions will require real understanding of what was read and will not allow the student to find the exact words of the response in the passage. Likewise, caution must be used lest the statements turn into an exercise of logic. Some of the test types which may be evolved from a written passage, and which are suitable for use at all levels, but particularly for beginners and intermediate students, are:

a) True-false questions.
b) Multiple-choice completion questions.

c) Multiple-choice answering questions dealing with content or with vocabulary comprehension.

With more advanced students, whose writing skill has been more perfected, and to a lesser degree with intermediate students, the question requiring a written answer, in a complete sentence, is a valid and useful test type. Again care must be taken that the questions are so constructed that the student cannot merely copy a statement from the reading passage for his answer. Here, however, Valette reminds us that two skills, reading and writing, are involved, and two grades probably should be assigned: one for correct content and one for correct form.[4]

VI. *Testing of Writing.* Again many of the pattern drill exercises discussed in Chapter 5 make excellent writing tests. Frequently the cues are given orally and the student is required to write the response. This procedure is not highly recommended, however, since it again involves two skills, and good testing techniques dictate that only one skill should be tested at any one time. It is therefore advisable to provide the student with the written stimulus to which he is to respond. Care must be taken not to construct items in which the response can be merely copied from the stimulus. At the risk of seeming repetitious, we include below some of the pattern drills which are effective testing devices:

1. *Substitution and/or correlation*

Vamos a la fiesta. (parque)
Catalina habló por teléfono. (Las dos jóvenes)
Mis amigos llegaron. (salir)

2. *Replacement*

For example, students are instructed to replace nouns with pronouns:

Prestó *el dinero a su primo.* (Se lo prestó.)

3. *Sentence completion* ("filling blanks")

a) Student completes a word or words:

El profesor no permitió que los estudiantes entr_____ en la aula.

---

[4] Rebecca Valette, *Modern Language Testing: A Handbook* (New York: Harcourt, Brace & World, 1967), pp. 126 ff. Many of the concepts presented here are based upon ideas set forth in this valuable book.

b) Student supplies necessary or appropriate words:

Dos, cuatro, _____, ocho, diez.

Vamos a la escuela a _____.

Pablo trató _____ hacerlo, pero no pudo.

> This type of exercise should *never* include a mixture of English and the target language. Such items as "Los dos muchachos _____ (have just left) la biblioteca" completely defeat the aims of audio-lingual instruction.

4. *Transformation*

El carpintero no puede ir.   (Change to the future tense)
El joven no duerme mucho.   (Change to the plural)
Las lecciones son largas.   (Change to the interrogative)

5. *Joining sentences*
This test assures the student's ability to use conjunctives and relators. Student is given two sentences to combine into one:

Enrique es mi amigo mexicano. Va a pasar un mes con mi familia.
(Enrique es mi amigo mexicano que va a pasar un mes con mi familia.)

Jorge no vino a la clase hoy. Se sentía mal.
(Jorge no vino a la clase hoy porque se sentía mal.)

6. *Directed response*

Dígale a su amiga que le va a dar un regalo. (Te voy a dar un regalo.)
Dígale al maestro que Vd. no puede ir. (No puedo ir.)
Pregúntele a Roberto si ha visto a Juana. (¿Has visto a Juana?)

7. *Directed question-response*, dealing with specific structures:

(Verb form): ¿Quieren Vds. tomar un refresco? (Sí, ...)
(Expression of time): ¿Cuánto tiempo hace que vive Vd. aquí? (Tres meses . . . .)
(*Gustar*): ¿A Vd. le gustan las manzanas? (No, ...)

8. *Construction of sentences*

One of the most effective methods of testing sentence structure is that of giving the student a group of words from which he is to construct a sentence using the words in the order given, and adding any words he may choose to enhance his sentence: Ayer / jóvenes / recibir / cartas.

Possible sentences: Ayer los jóvenes recibieron muchas cartas.
Ayer los jóvenes no recibieron cartas.
Ayer las jóvenes recibieron tres cartas.
Etc.

When a specific point of structure is to be tested in this type of test, a model sentence is frequently given with the instruction that the student is to construct a similar sentence with the words provided:

Lo compré ayer.
La / ver / mañana.
(La veré mañana.)

9. *Passage transformation*

Students are provided with a printed passage in which they are to change all verbs to the appropriate past tense, or to substitute all nouns with pronouns, etc.

10. *Definitions* (already discussed under section IV above).

¿En qué escribe Vd. los ejercicios?   (un cuaderno)

11. *Dialogue writing*

Students are given a narrative passage describing a situation in which two (or more) persons are involved. Students are then instructed to write a possible dialogue between the persons, discussing the content of the narrative.

A variation of this type is provided by giving the student a dialogue and instructing him to write a narrative involving the content of the dialogue.

12. *Composition*

The composition test in which students are asked to compose passages of related sentences on a given topic is widely used, but but it is also frequently misused. Grading tends to be less objective; often two teachers reading the same composition will assign different grades, since frequently the grade is based on some sort of overall impression.

Therefore, the teacher who assigns a composition as a testing device should have two or three objectives in mind, and the grading should be based on the student's performance in these areas. The teacher should also remember that certain points of structure can be better tested by some of the types discussed above; therefore, the composition should be judged on aspects not covered in more objective tests. Some of the objectives which could be evaluated on a composition might be:

a) Breadth of student's vocabulary; amount of recall.
b) Use of modifiers. (Students might be asked to describe a picture or an imaginary scene, or to write a narrative involving a great deal of action which would elicit abundant adverbial modifiers.)
c) Use of verbs, in assigned tenses.
d) Grammatical points, such as the use of conditional tense in the composition topic: "What would you do if school were dismissed for the remainder of today?"

All the foregoing discussion deals with writing tests which have written stimuli, but we must not overlook writing tests which utilize oral cues. As was said earlier, these are recommended more for testing speaking and comprehension, but they may be used for testing writing, provided certain features are maintained. First, the content must be familiar to all students. Second, the teacher must determine how he will score the results. Again it must be stated that a student who scores low in listening comprehension tests might be able to write well, but if he fails to comprehend the oral stimulus on this type of test, his written response will also be incorrect and his score in writing has suffered. The teacher must, therefore, consider the following in scoring written responses to oral stimuli: a) Does the student's response show that he understood the meaning of the oral cue? b) Are his errors ones of structure, meaning, or a lack of comprehension? Here again, it might be well to assign two grades on this type of test.

The dictations and guided writing exercises are two of the most widely used test types with oral stimuli and have been extensively discussed in Chapter 7.

Another common type is that in which the student responds in some way to a passage which is read orally. The passage should be read twice, and the test questions should be read twice. The students must respond in Spanish. Possible student responses include the following:

a) Writing a summary of the passage, or retelling it.
b) Writing answers to multiple-choice questions presented orally. The question is read as an incomplete statement with four (or more) possible completions. Students select and then write the proper answer. For example, for a passage about the problems the García family had in deciding about a proposed trip, the question might be:

"Según el autor, los señores García . . ."

    A) no quieren hacer el viaje por auto.

    B) no pueden hacer el viaje porque está descompuesto su coche.

    C) creen que resultaría más barato ir por tren.

    D) no van a menos que los acompañen sus hijos.

VII. *Testing of cultural information.* Where this is skillfully worked into the audio-lingual text or elsewhere, it need not constitute a separate unit of study. It can be tested in both a linguistic and a situational context. This can be accomplished in several ways, of which the two more widely preferred are the multiple-choice completion items based on a resumptive reading selection (that is, a reading selection combining in new ways material already learned by the pupils) and a rearranging or matching exercise in which the student reorganizes the sentences in a paragraph to demonstrate his control of the material.

Those teachers who teach a civilization-culture course in the last year of their sequences would do well to consult books on language testing. Robert Lado has a section on testing of cross-cultural understanding where he suggests several testing techniques including the following multiple-choice format:

Situation: A soccer match is in progress in Spain. There is a moment of fast action in front of one of the goals. Most of the spectators stand up and WHISTLE LOUDLY. They are:

    (1) showing enthusiastic approval of the play.

    (2) showing displeasure.

    (3) showing relief after a moment of danger.

    (4) asking for a repetition; more of the same.

    (5) signaling the end of the game.[5]

Frequent short testing of specific skills (one at a time), tightly linked to the lesson plan, is more productive than widely spaced, all-encompassing tests. Any test loses its value for the student unless it is corrected immediately. Immediate correction can sometimes be achieved by the carbon paper technique mentioned in Chapter 7, by the use of the overhead projector, by going over the test orally, or by giving each student a corrected copy.

When skills are mixed on a test, it is difficult to grade accurately and to weigh the parts of the test so they are proportionate to the emphasis

---

[5] Robert Lado, *Language Testing*, p. 286, © 1965 by McGraw-Hill Book Company, and reprinted with their permission.

given the skill in class work. Therefore, when tests are desired which test all skills, it is better to use those prepared (and statistically scored) by competent agencies such as the MLA, ETS, and CEEB, all of which have national norms. These tests, the use of which has been too limited in high schools to date, will be mentioned again in Chapter 11.

Where a school is unable to obtain such prepared examinations and seeks to devise its own, the following type of examination, which has been used successfully, may be a useful model. For such an examination, an entirely new kind of test item had to be devised. It was nearly impossible to compress even so little as a single question on each of the more than 140 grammatical focuses of a first-level audio-lingual text (not to mention the pronunciation drills, cultural readings, etc.) into a two- or three-hour examination given at one time or spread over two or three days. First, it was generally agreed to test the students' speaking ability separately in the laboratory prior to the final examination, for reasons we have already touched upon above. The remaining skills, reading, writing, and comprehension, are left for the comprehensive examination. The test is divided into two parts, one involving the tape recorder and the other, straightforward writing. The first part is subsequently sub-divided into two equal halves. The first half consists of a series of questions read twice at normal speed on the tape by native speakers (as many different dialects as possible are represented, and male and female voices are used), for which the students are required to choose the best of four possible answers (given in their test booklets). The second half reverses the procedure, and the taped portion consists of statements read twice. The students are to choose which of the four questions given in their booklets most likely would elicit the answer they just heard. Within each of these two halves of the first part of the test, the items are so constructed that in approximately two-thirds of them the correct answer differs from the incorrect ones for structural reasons. Of course, all items are in correct Spanish; three choices simply do not answer the question. In the other third of the items in each half, the correct answer is determined by the cultural content. Thus, both aural comprehension and understanding of cultural material, and the passive recognition of structure and ability to read rapidly and accurately are tested in a single set of items.

The second part of the test is entirely written. The items are of the pattern drill type, in which students are required to demonstrate their active control of structural patterns and their ability to read the language.

For the individual high school teacher, however, such a procedure of test construction and administration is very difficult. His solution to the resumptive or comprehensive testing problem lies in the judicious selection of "key" structural and cultural points to be tested. Then he may proceed to the careful construction of test items on these points.

A chapter on testing would not be complete without some treatment of methods of scoring, item analysis, and statistical evaluation. Valette has provided an excellent discussion of these aspects of foreign language testing;[6] it is our purpose here only to touch briefly on major considerations.

It must be stressed that the teacher is obliged to give ample thought to the method of scoring, the number of possible errors, point values to be assigned and weighted importance of various items when the test is being constructed. He must decide carefully what aspect is being tested in any item or set of items and develop a consistent method of scoring to accompany the items.

Of course, nothing needs to be said about the scoring of true-false, matching or multiple-choice items, since the choice is clearly correct or incorrect and it is easy to see that a student gave four incorrect answers out of a possible ten, thus achieving a 60% proficiency.

If, however, a pattern drill is used as a testing device, the scoring may become somewhat more complicated or refined. It is recommended that one point be assigned to each substitution or transformation involved. Thus, "Voy a la biblioteca. Juan _____." would be worth one point, since it involves only the change of the verb form. If there are further changes in structure in the item, more points should be granted. Thus, "Escribo una carta a mi padre. Nosotros _____." could have two possible errors and thus two points ("Nosotros escribimos una carta a nuestro padre"). But whether each possible error is assigned a point value of 1, $\frac{1}{2}$, or any other number, is of little consequence. What is important is that whatever system is devised, it should be systematically applied to all items.

In scoring a dictation the same consistency is essential. Some teachers prefer to count the total number of words in the passage, regardless of difficulty, and use this total as the maximum possible score. For each incorrect or omitted word, one point is then subtracted. Others subtract only $\frac{1}{2}$ point for a word which is recognizable but misspelled, but still assign a value of one point to an omitted word. Still others choose to refine it even more by using one of the above systems, but subtracting only $\frac{1}{4}$ point for an omitted or incorrect diacritical mark and not count the entire word as an error. Another suggested method for scoring dictations is to divide the sentences into words and/or phrases

---

[6] *Modern Language Testing*, Chapter IV, and pp. 134–137.

of somewhat equal difficulty and give equal point values to each division.[7]

Every teacher will have evolved his own system for deciding what letter grades should be assigned to the various scores on any given test, but some knowledge of methods of statistical evaluation can be of great use to the teacher in this process. A sheet should be prepared with the test scores arranged in rank order from the highest to the lowest. From this the teacher can quickly see the range and distribution of scores, and he can compute the mean, median, etc. An accumulation of scores at either end of the range, a noticeable lack of high scores, even from his best students, will indicate to the teacher that some adjustment in assigning letter grades may be necessary, but even more important, it will give the teacher reason to question the validity and reliability of his test (unless, of course, the class is comprised only of high-achievers, low-achievers, etc.).

Another very useful mechanism is an item analysis of the test items. By tallying the number of errors made on each item, the teacher readily sees which items proved most difficult for the class as a whole. He can then review the items to see whether they were faulty or whether the point being tested had not yet been thoroughly mastered by the class and should therefore be reviewed or retaught in subsequent class sessions.

On multiple-choice objective tests, the analysis must be more detailed. A tally sheet similar to the following has been recommended by Valette (p. 39):

Item Number	Response			
	A	B	C	D
1	II	⦿ ⦿ (𝔥𝔥𝔥 III)	III	III
2	I	III	(𝔥𝔥𝔥 𝔥𝔥𝔥)	II
3	III	(𝔥𝔥𝔥 I)	𝔥𝔥𝔥 I	I
4	(𝔥𝔥𝔥 𝔥𝔥𝔥 𝔥𝔥𝔥)	I		
5	IIII	IIII	IIII	(IIII)

---

[7] The point values given here have been suggested by Valette, *op. cit.*, p. 137.

The correct answer for each item has been circled. Items 1, 2, and 4 indicate a normal performance. Item 3 deserves careful scrutiny since an equal number of students chose B and C. Perhaps the item was badly worded, directions were not clear, or both B and C were possible answers, which would indicate faulty item construction. Or it is possible that a rather fine point was being tested and the students as a whole were not yet able to distinguish between two closely related, but unidentical, responses. Item 5 indicates that there may be something wrong with the test item rather than with the student. The item should be discarded and not counted on this test.

In conclusion, it may be said that plans for evaluation and scoring of a test are an essential part of test construction, and that item analysis after the test is a vital function in judging the results. A test may be considered, after all, not only a means to measure the students' performance, but also a device which every good language teacher uses to evaluate his own effectiveness and to help him determine those aspects needing more emphasis in his planning for the course.

A System for Oral Production Testing in the Classroom
by Gustave Mathieu

Equipment requirements are as follows:

1. A tape recorder with an output or monitor jack.
2. An adaptor which can be plugged into the output or monitor jack and into which can be plugged two sets of headphones. In other words, an adaptor which converts a single output jack into a double output jack. (The type of adaptor one will need will depend upon the type of tape recorder used.)

Schematic:

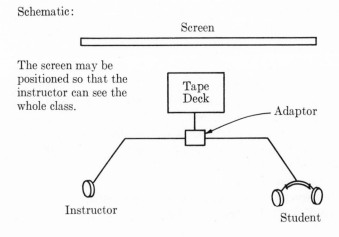

3. Two sets of headphones — one a standard set, the other modified for one-ear listening.
4. A screen which shields the student and his voice from the rest of the class.
5. The test tape.

All the equipment should be tested before the first student is tested and the volume should be adjusted to a comfortable level. Using the "one-eared" headphone the instructor is able to hear all that the student hears in addition to the student's response — this eliminates the need for a microphone and an additional amplifier.

The tape may contain only one or many copies of the test. In the first case the tape must be rewound after testing each student; in the second case the number of rewindings is reduced but the amount of time required to produce the tape is increased. In either case the tape should have a long leader attached to avoid having to rethread the tape after rewinding.

Sample Echo Test

The echo test consists of two parts: (1) a taped passage to be repeated phrase by phrase by the student on the "record" track of the tape, and (2) a set of evaluative criteria by which the teacher judges the student's performance. The taped passage is best selected from the reading materials used during the semester. It should be spoken at normal speed, preferably by a native speaker. The evaluative criteria need not all be applied at once to a given reading. Thus, the teacher may prefer to evaluate the student on his performance in only one or two of the areas at a time.

The following are the major evaluative criteria:

1. Inaccurate formation of vowel sounds (possibly English influences as in [ɪ] for [i], etc.)
2. Lengthening of stressed syllables
3. Diphthongizing Spanish vowels under stress ([léy] for [le])
4. Dissolution of diphthongs
5. Deformation of semivowels and semiconsonants by giving them the character of hiatus groups ([bɛndió] for [bɛndjó])
6. Retroflection of consonants
7. Aspiration of stops
8. Incorrect voicing ([prezénte] for [presénte])
9. Labiodental [v] for [b] or [β]

10. Omissions
11. Incorrect syllabication (breaths between words instead of between phonological phrases)
12. Incorrect accentuation ([él ló íso] for [eloíso] *él lo hizo*)

Different numerical or letter grade values may be assigned to the criteria being used during a given test. It is frequently helpful to determine the number of potential errors of a given type in a given passage and then to grade in the form of a fraction made up of the student's errors over the number of possible errors, e.g., 15 stressed syllables of which the student lengthened 6, yielding the grade of $\frac{6}{15}$. In this way, the same test given at specific intervals throughout the semester will give the teacher a good idea of the progress a student may be making in pronunciation.

▶ EXERCISES

1. Discuss what you understand by "normal language behavior" in the following statement made in this chapter: "Collective measurement (all four skills) gives us a practical index of achievement for communication goals so long as that complex of skills required on the examination is natural in *normal language behavior*."
2. Discuss the advantages and disadvantages of short tests of specific skills as opposed to the more comprehensive tests.
3. In Chapter 6 there is a list of "do's and dont's" for the use of the language laboratory. Prepare a list, for discussion, of the "dont's" in the preparation of audio-lingual tests.
4. Why is the immediate correction of a test in keeping with the principles upon which the fundamental skills approach is based?
5. Discuss the advantages and disadvatages of the use of standardized national tests such as those suggested in this chapter.
6. Discuss the use of English in foreign language testing.
7. What testing techniques may be used to replace the traditional translation questions?
8. What special characteristic of the structural behavior of *por* and *para* makes it difficult to test students on their active control of these forms, without resorting to translation? Do you think the testing of the comparative usage of these two forms might be accomplished by one or another of the vocabulary and idiom test patterns? Why or why not? Construct a brief *por* as against *para* quiz on this basis. Can you think of other structural items that may be better tested as vocabulary items? Why?

REFERENCE BOOKS AND ARTICLES

CARROLL, JOHN. "The Prediction of Success in Intensive Foreign Language Teaching" (New York: MLA, 1966).

———— et al. *Modern Language Aptitude Test* (New York: The Psychological Corp., 1959).

DELATTRE, PIERRE. "Testing Students' Progress in the Language Laboratory" (*Automated Teaching Bulletin* I, 1960), 21–31.

EATON, ESTHER. "Evaluation and Testing in Teaching Modern Foreign Languages" (*School Life* XLIV, 1962), 19–22.

LADO, ROBERT. *Language Testing* (New York: McGraw-Hill, 1965).

PIMSLEUR, PAUL. "Testing Foreign Language Learning," in Albert Valdman, ed., *Trends in Language Teaching* (New York: McGraw-Hill, 1965).

SCHEVILL, KARL. "Means for Evaluation of Language Learning" (*California Schools* XXXI, 1960), 117–121.

STARR, WILMARTH. "Proficiency Tests in Modern Foreign Languages" (*PMLA* LXXVI, 1961), 7–11.

VALETTE, REBECCA. *Modern Language Testing* (New York: Harcourt, Brace & World, 1967).

Two useful references listing foreign language tests of the type discussed in this chapter are:

BUROS, OSCAR. *Mental Measurements Yearbook* (Highland Park, New Jersey: Gryphon Press, 1965).

————. *Tests in Print* (Highland Park, New Jersey: Gryphon Press, 1961).

Some of the more widely used tests in Spanish programs are:

Carroll-Sapon Modern Language Aptitude Test (New York: Psychological Corp., 1959).

Pimsleur Language Aptitude Battery (New York: Harcourt, Brace & World, 1966).

Common Concepts Foreign Language Test (Monterey: California Test Bureau, 1962).

MLA Cooperative Foreign Language Tests (Princeton: Educational Testing Service, 1963).

Pimsleur Modern Foreign Language Proficiency Tests (New York: Harcourt, Brace & World, 1967).

College Board Advanced Placement Tests (Princeton: Educational Testing Service, 1968).

9

*S*electing and adapting audio-lingual textbooks

Despite the fact that the first widespread commercial appearance of textbooks implementing the audio-lingual approach took place shortly after the war, when the intensive training texts developed for the military were adapted for college use and released, the current deluge of supposedly audio-lingual texts was largely triggered by the experience of many teachers in the NDEA summer institute programs. The result is that while today's foreign language teacher has a wider variety of modern materials to choose from than ever before he is confronted with a far more serious and complex problem of selection.[1] Many teachers, after deciding to adopt the audio-lingual approach, have selected what was advertised as an audio-lingual textbook, only to find their efforts and sometimes the success of their entire program undermined by inconsistent and frequently unteachable texts. Upon closer examination, the text is often recognized either as a traditional one, hurriedly and superficially revised to give the appearance of implementing audio-lingual instruction, or as a new production, prepared by writers who are well-meaning but insufficiently experienced in audio-lingual techniques. Still others have found themselves in the difficult position of having to teach along audio-lingual lines with purely traditional materials. Thus,

---

[1] Some of the more widely known audio-lingual texts are listed at the end of Chapter 2.

the modern language teacher is confronted with a dual problem with regard to textbooks: how to select one for use in the audio-lingual class, and how to adapt a traditional text for such use when no modern text is available.[2]

Selecting an Audio-lingual Text

As a matter of principle, where possible, it is always better to acquire a text especially designed for audio-lingual instruction than to adapt unsuitable ones.

The exact set of criteria by which any textbook is judged varies from school to school and from teacher to teacher. Frequently, a major consideration is the number of units needed to present a certain percentage of the course, so that it may be completed within a semester, year, or other length of time. Other considerations may reflect the need for more pictures and "fun" content, e.g., for junior high school pupils, while a more direct approach is sufficient for the high school pupil. Thus, it would be impossible for us to give here a universal list of the requirements a text should fulfill in order to be useful in the fundamental skills approach. In general, we may say that the most successful text is likely to be the one which most closely corresponds to the organization of the audio-lingual lesson, as we have described and discussed it in earlier chapters. The center of any audio-lingual text is its drills. Therefore, the bulk of a unit should be made up of a variety of drills covering the major grammatical focuses in the lesson. The criteria established for meaningful syntactical drills in Chapter 5 should be applied rigorously in evaluating the pattern drill sections of each unit. The two consistent questions must be: (1) does this drill do the job? and (2) are there sufficient drills to make this structure automatic in the student?

At least one example of all structural types and of new vocabulary items and idioms to be drilled should be presented to the student in the form of a dialogue at the beginning of the unit. Sometimes, especially in more advanced stages, a prose selection is used in place of a dialogue. Although a book which prefers the reading selection to the dialogue is not always to be discounted on that consideration alone, the dialogue performs specific, unique functions (as we have discussed) so important

---

[2] Discussions of lesson plans, use of drills, testing, etc. found in teachers' manuals accompanying audio-lingual texts may serve as useful guides for the teacher faced with the problem of adapting a traditional text. (Cf. Teachers' manuals for *Modern Spanish, A-LM Spanish;* Michalski's *Spanish: Oral Approach;* the Staubach-Walsh *First Year Spanish,* revised edition; and the Staubach-Eldon-Walsh *Second Year Spanish,* revised edition.)

that its omission at least at the beginning level, is a serious defect. The linguistic and cultural authenticity of each dialogue and reading selection must be beyond question. Explanations of grammar should *follow* the inductive drills. Students should be provided with a recombination narrative or dialogue adaptation at the end of the unit, or a combined pattern replacement drill to serve as a means of tying the lesson together. Extensive use of prose passages to be translated, vocabulary and idiom lists, and exercises requiring the pupil to use forms out of context (verb conjugations, declensions, etc.), or the use of half-Spanish, half-English utterances are general indications that a book is unsuitable for the audio-lingual program.

Some texts are published with tapes of the dialogues and drill material. *Modern Spanish*, for example, comes with filmed versions of the dialogues. Others have correlated visual aids. Bull's *Visual Grammar* may be acquired to provide visual accompaniment to almost any audio-lingual text.

It is important, then, that the foreign language teacher be knowledgeable in the selection, evaluation, and utilization of modern audio-visual resources in order to incorporate them to maximum advantage in the audio-lingual teaching plan. We shall discuss the primary uses of motion pictures, slides, and filmstrips in teaching the sociocultural context in Chapter 10. It should be noted here, however, that many modern texts have their dialogues and some drills on film. This technique assists the student in associating the language patterns he is learning with visually stimulated, real-life situations without recourse to translation. Because of the cost of production of movies, slides, and filmstrips, however, most teachers would be well advised to make use of those which have been prepared professionally. Most teachers will find that the overhead projector will provide them with the opportunity for creating specific visual aids for the language learning sequence both inexpensively and efficiently.[3]

The presence of a teacher's manual can be very important. Of course, there are valuable textbooks which do not have such manuals and it is likewise true that such manuals can be too detailed or rigid to take into full account the classroom situations which vary from school to school.

---

[3] Some of the uses of the overhead projector in the foreign language classroom have been discussed by Karl Pond, "A Language Teaching Tool: The Overhead Projector" (*The Modern Language Journal* XLVII, 1963), 30–33. Additional uses of the motion picture in similar contexts are discussed by Anna Lottmann, "Films in the Modern Language Class" (*The Modern Language Journal* XLV, 1961), 178–180; and F. B. Creore, "The New Media in Language Teaching" (*Audio-Visual Instruction* V, 1960), 286–293.

Moreover, the teacher himself will need to determine between following the manual exactly and exercising professional initiative and imagination, provided that these are based on sound principles of language teaching. At their best, these manuals provide invaluable suggestions for the implementation of each lesson, the transition from skill to skill, lesson plans, suggested testing routines, and suggestions for classroom procedures. The manuals accompanying the *A-LM* series are excellent, as is the teacher's edition of the *Entender y Hablar* series.

Each unit of the prospective text should contain each of the elements of the audio-lingual lesson as described on pp. 20–26. If a book is deficient in any one of the areas represented in the outline, the teacher risks reduced efficiency in the program in which the book is to be used.

Many texts come with accompanying workbooks. If the printed lesson in the main text is incomplete, however, the workbook may not always be a sufficient supplement for real teaching efficiency. Ideally, the workbook, if present, should provide the student with extra opportunities for reinforcement, practice, and advancement at home and in the laboratory rather than take the place of the fundamental drills which each unit in the text should otherwise provide.

Adapting a Traditional Text

For many teachers, however, the problem is not one of choosing among several new audio-lingual texts and evaluating their relative merits. Rather, they have to make do in an audio-lingual program with a traditional text or a slipshod "audio-lingual" text, which suffers from many, if not all, the defects we have just mentioned. Now let us consider the steps to be taken in order to adapt such a deficient text to the needs of the truly audio-lingual class.

1. *The "hear-speak-read-write" order.* This is the underlying principle of sequential learning. Regardless of how the textbook presents its material, adapting it to the audio-lingual classroom implies strict adherence to that order.

2. *Aural presentation vs. audio-lingual presentation.* Too often, the conscientious teacher, in his efforts to present a traditional text audio-lingually, will read the patterns to be studied to his class, making the students listen and give some evidence of comprehension. This is an inadequate presentation, because it is entirely aural and denies the pupil the opportunity to practice speaking what he has just heard. The audio-lingual presentation always implies that the student participates actively in the hearing-speaking exercise.

Some teachers devote a period of weeks — or even an entire semester

— to the "prereading phase" ("prereading" as opposed to a "textbook phase," using the former term to refer to the time spent on presenting the structures in the traditional textbook aurally to the students and requiring them to practice them audio-lingually and to memorize them). During this pre-reading period the student does not see the textbook but performs all language activity from the basis presented orally by the teacher in class. This technique can be truly satisfactory only when the material used comes from a scientifically designed, audio-lingual text. Only in such texts can the teacher be assured of the careful structuring of material so that the correct percentages of new material, review, drill, etc., are present to sustain a semester of purely aural-oral linguistic experience. Despite widespread belief to the contrary, it is safer for the teacher who must continue to use a less than adequate text to make use of a pre-reading phase, as suggested above, preliminary to each unit to be studied, rather than to prepare a pre-reading semester or year from inadequate materials.

3. *Reworking the text.* Because most traditional texts make no attempt to present the patterns to be studied in any kind of contextual dialogue, the teacher's first responsibility is to provide the pupils with a substitute. This is what is often meant by the pre-reading phase of each unit or chapter. To begin with, the teacher must make a careful inventory of the structural and lexical content of each chapter. This inventory most often takes the form of a list, including the grammatical points to be taught in the lesson; the associated vocabulary, idioms, and common expressions; and cultural points to be induced. At the same time, the teacher must make an estimate of the amount of time that can be spent on that lesson within the scope of the semester. Of that total time, approximately 40% to 50% should be spent on the pre-reading phase of each lesson throughout the first two years, when authentic basic dialogues are not present.

The teacher must then select from the text, or compose, basic pattern sentences which contain all the structural items used in the body of the lesson for drill. It is always better to select items from prepared materials, however, for reasons we have discussed. Vocabulary, because there is usually so much of it in a lesson, should not constitute individual focuses for pattern sentences (idioms excluded), but as much of the new vocabulary as possible should be worked into the pattern sentences. This is a large and complex task, best accomplished when a committee of all the teachers of the various sections of the course work together. It is always necessary to submit these pattern sentences to native speakers to insure their colloquial authenticity. As we have said before, these pattern sentences should be incorporated into a brief dialogue consisting of approximately ten utterances involving two or three speakers as a satisfactory minimum. These utterances are to be memorized and treated as would be the dialogue in the audio-lingual text. Where the teacher's command of the target language is obviously non-native, he should attempt to have a native speaker record the dialogues on tape for use in class. If the teacher is unable to construct a natural dialogue, then the following slightly less effective alternative is suggested: Basic pattern sentences would be presented in no particular order for the purpose of audio-lingual drill; the sentences would be memorized; the first practice goal would be to elicit action responses to nonverbal cues, followed by a reworking into questions and answers; then responses to a directed dialogue in a progressive development of structure and vocabulary would be required.

4. *Dialogue-drill sequence.* It should be noted that, since the dialogues suggested above are short, it may take three or four separate dialogues to present all the structures of a given unit. If this is the case, it is best to drill the structures presented in each dialogue after it is learned. Since the purpose of the dialogue is to present the patterns for drill, the drills must not be postponed for long after the basic sentences are memorized and drilled. Thus, each day's lesson must be planned as a unit for presentation, including a check-up, exercises, and review of the memorized dialogue, plus some drill on at least one, and preferably two or three of the basic pattern sentences. The result may well be that the revised lesson will not correspond to any lesson divisions in the original source text. A systematic review of the dialogues should be scheduled at fairly frequent intervals, perhaps every fifth meeting. The more difficult constructions should reappear most frequently in the dialogues and should be the object of recurring review drills.

5. *Improvised warm-up.* This "all-business" approach may need to be modified somewhat for the junior high school and for certain high school classes by the judicious use of supplementary material. The purpose of such supplementary material is to provide more of what might be called a "foreign language atmosphere." The most economical way of achieving this is by teaching the students a set of daily routine phrases, such as greetings, simple and often-used instructions, and the like. For some pupils, the use of Spanish names is helpful in promoting a predisposition to speak Spanish. Other classes react favorably to a few moments at the beginning of the period devoted to describing what one member of the class is wearing or a picture placed in front of the class. The dangerous element here is simply that too much time (more than five minutes) spent on this activity robs the pupils of their opportunity to learn the language. Consequently, such activities should be

used only where necessary for the specific purpose of setting a mood for the serious business of the hour.

6. *The pattern drill phase.* Once a unit has been introduced through dialogue and practice with the basic sentences, the student must be drilled on the use of the structures presented. This involves a process of selection, since texts not audio-lingually oriented tend to present at widely separated points various aspects of a single structural phenomenon and fail to make clear the application of the "rules" they give. Almost always, the generalization precedes the exercises, and often the only exercises included in a series of units are translations from Spanish into English and the reverse.

Thus, the teacher faces two important tasks from the very beginning: one, to select the content of each day's lesson with a view toward fixing the basic speech habits most essential for developing audio-lingual competence; and two, to reorganize much of that material. As the course progresses, the content of the structural patterns presented becomes more complex. Generally, the rate of introduction of new vocabulary and idioms increases as the lessons progress. As this happens, a constantly growing percentage of that material is required for reading recognition or aural comprehension only. In this way, a transition is achieved from an emphasis on aural-oral skills to one on reading and writing. The difficulty is that, whereas in audio-lingual texts this transition is accomplished only after aural-oral competence has been thoroughly established, in many traditional texts the reading and writing skills become paramount and are led into after perhaps only three or four lessons. The teacher faced with the problem of adapting such materials will have to convert many of the early reading-writing portions of the traditional text to audio-lingual presentation and drill.

In the secondary school, most Spanish programs never get around to considering such things as style. Thus, for the purposes of adapting a text for audio-lingual use, the teacher must be certain to include the most often reoccurring structures, high-frequency vocabulary items, and idioms. This task is made even more difficult by the absence of an up-to-date scientific study indicating the range and frequency of the most commonly used words and structures in modern spoken Spanish. Of those studies which are available, the following five are the most reliable:

Ismael Rodríguez Bou and Juana Méndez, eds., *Recuento de vocabulario español* (Consejo Superior de Enseñanza de Puerto Rico, 1952).

Milton A. Buchanan, *A Graded Spanish Word Book* (Toronto: University of Toronto Press, 1927).

Hayward Keniston, *Spanish Syntax List* (New York: Holt, 1937).

Hayward Keniston, *A Standard List of Basic Words and Idioms* (Boston: D.C. Heath, 1941).

Víctor García Hoz, *Vocabulario usual, común y fundamental* (Madrid: CSIC, 1953).

It is on the basis of the range and frequency tabulation in these works that the initial order of presentation and subsequent reappearances of structures and words are based.

Once it is decided that a given vocabulary or structural item is to be presented in an audio-lingual lesson, the teacher must select a set of expressions incorporating them. These expressions must be restricted to the important items of the lesson, must be presentable through pattern drills or conversational sequences that are challenging to the level of the student — and therefore representative of progression in the learning process — yet must be understandable to him within the context of the lesson (and, of course, what has gone before). Such selected items should then be presented in a series — generally a dialogue — in accordance with principles we have already examined. Of course, important new words can be used with review structures, and new structures with review vocabulary or idioms, but *always* within the restriction that the meaning of these new forms can be inferred. We shall have more to say about the techniques of teaching students to infer meaning in Chapter 12.

Frequently, the more recently published traditional texts utilize the dialogue form in conversational sequences. (Such use of dialogue is, as we have seen, no sure indication that the rest of a text is audio-lingually designed.) Where this is the case, the basic pattern sentences may generally be taken directly from the text. In general, though, traditional texts do not provide a comprehensive set of pattern sentences. Moreover, they often list much low-frequency vocabulary and dated or highly restricted regional idioms. In these instances, basic pattern sentences in situational context will have to be composed by the teacher.

There is really no single prescribed manner to present all structure and vocabulary audio-lingually. For structural exercise, one must use the various drills we discussed in Chapter 5. Vocabulary and idioms from the new lessons may be presented audio-lingually when their meanings can be illustrated or inferred. It is best when the teacher is able to assist such inferences by visual aids. The presentation may be combined with the structure drills for that particular lesson or may take the form of a series of drills, perhaps beginning with a repetition drill and followed by transformation, substitution, or completion drills.

Some Criteria for Textbook Evaluation

1. Does the text being evaluated adhere to the format of presentation recommended for well-designed audio-lingual materials?
2. Does the format of each unit correspond to the needs of four-skill presentation? (Presents material for developing the listening comprehension and speaking skills before introducing the reading and writing skills.)
3. Are correlated tape recordings available?
4. Are correlated visual aids available?
5. Is there a complete teacher's manual for each level with specific information and guidelines for the presentation of each type of language learning activity?
6. Does the first level lead on to other levels in an articulated series which is methodologically unified?
7. Is the language usage representative of the spoken language of educated native speakers of the same linguistic age as those represented in the dialogues or of the students at the level for which the book is designed?
8. Is the drill material adequate to habituate the language patterns presented?
9. Is material reviewed and recalled systematically throughout?
10. Are test frames or actual sample tests included in the book or teacher's manual?
11. Is the cultural information presented in the book scrupulously accurate?
12. Is there an accompanying workbook or other supplementary exercises for additional reinforcement and practice when needed?
13. Is the overall "tone" of the book attractive to the level of student for which it is designed?
14. Does each unit contain a section in which the student is able to perform the specific language skills taught in the unit in a new, but analogous, context?
15. Is supplementary reading material included, and is it appropriate to the level of the text?
16. Are writing exercises included, and do they progress through the recommended phases at a steady rate?

▶ EXERCISES

1. Discuss in detail the specific criteria you would use to select an audio-lingual text for your school's Spanish program. Base your judgment on the earlier chapters of this book as well as the present

one. If possible, bring to class an audio-lingual text of the type you would choose and illustrate your conclusions with it.

2. If you are now using an audio-lingual text, discuss those features in it which correspond to the criteria suggested in this chapter. Also discuss the advantages or disadvantages of those features which are not among those described here. If you now use a traditional text, discuss the possibilities of adapting it for audio-lingual use.

3. Discuss how the presence of a correlated tape or visual program for a given text does not in itself guarantee that the text is audio-lingually conceived.

4. Discuss the relative advantages of withholding the printed text from the pupils during specific phases of instruction at the beginning levels.

5. Discuss how the authors of audio-lingual books systematically increment the presentation of new vocabulary and idioms to correspond to the linguistic needs of each successive unit, while at the same time building toward the broad active and passive vocabulary required for free conversation, free composition, and extensive reading.

10

Teaching the cultural context

Although speaking a foreign language fluently is our major goal in the foreign language program, it is still not *all* we aim to teach. In addition, the pupil needs to know something of the way of life and the intellectual and artistic products of the culture whose language he is studying. This should be one of the results of the pupil's experience in the foreign language course. It is important to tell the student clearly that not only do the phonology, morphology, and syntax of the language he is studying differ from his own but also that the images which these forms call up for the native speaker are totally different. This is one of the most important functions of the total language program.

Does the audio-lingual approach minimize cultural information in the classroom as is sometimes claimed and, therefore, fail to fulfill this larger function of language teaching? The conflict is more apparent than real. It is based on a misinterpretation of the phrase *"total* language program." The audio-lingual approach teaches us that the hearing, speaking, reading, and writing skills must be perfected before the student may turn his attention from manipulating forms to the reading and discussion of cultural concepts. We have learned that in the complex matter of language it is essential to divide language into separate parts, or "skills," so as to teach each one thoroughly, yet not lose sight of the innate relationship among them and of the overriding fact that people talk and write in order to communicate ideas.

The modern approach recognizes that a genuine understanding of Hispanic culture — a sympathetic comprehension of the problems of its people and a familiarity with their cultural patterns, based upon a background of factual information — is an integral part of the total language program, but that pedagogical emphases vary at different points within that total program. Thus, our very first concern is to teach the language skills. We never lose sight of the social context in which the forms are presented and drilled, but our major emphasis at first must be on the skills themselves. Then, to an ever-increasing degree as the student acquires greater fluency, our emphasis shifts to the cultural aspect of what the student speaks and writes about.

In the audio-lingual approach, the language itself, from the very beginning, is an intimate manifestation of culture, since it is at once the means of communication among the people who speak it and the fabric of which their very thoughts are formed. Thus, in equal degrees, the linguistic elements of culture are taught as part of language learning and nonlinguistic aspects of culture are used as vehicles for language learning. What we shall discuss in this chapter will be how we may most successfully integrate "language" and "culture" for the eventual purpose of teaching the student the total language, or as much of it as the finite learning situation in the secondary school will permit.

During the first two or three years of language instruction, the emphasis is on acquiring language skills. Thus, the same inductive approach that we use in presenting and drilling these skills is used for introducing the pupil to culture.

The first step in this inductive presentation of culture is achieved through the classroom environment itself. The Spanish classroom should set the stage for the serious business of language learning by focusing the student's attention as far as possible on things Spanish. Pictures, posters, objets d'art, and other visual material appropriate to the course (including visual aids which accompany many audiolingual texts) help to achieve this purpose. These visual aids should represent both historical and contemporary features of Spanish and Hispanic-American culture. Pupils who have collected or made materials of this sort should be encouraged to display them. In this way, an atmosphere conducive to a "Spanish frame of mind" is created, and a small but significant opportunity to begin the inductive approach to culture is given without taking time from the beginning class in its fundamental work of acquiring the language skills. Where it is at all possible to set aside classrooms exclusively for use by Spanish classes, more elaborate permanent displays can be prepared. A congenial atmosphere for language learning seems to be best achieved when language classes are not required to migrate from one end of the building to another or to share the scenery with the periodic table or dead frogs.

Second, the well-designed audio-lingual textbook is, from the first lesson on, an experience in both language *and* culture. The basic dialogue, as we have mentioned before, is a lesson in culture as well as language because it is an authentic example of the foreign language in context. Such context is by definition an authentic culture pattern. Any dialogue picked from *Modern Spanish*, second edition, for example, will illustrate this point. Dialogue 13 (pp. 205–206) is typical. The grammatical focuses of the dialogue include prepositional pronouns, negation by negative adverbs, comparison with *que*, and the like. But its cultural content is no less significant. Here, the pupil is introduced to one of the most striking features of Latin-American civilization: student concern for national politics. The American pupil can compare his own avid interest in sports with his Latin-American contemporary's interest in politics. He discovers that students in Latin America learn to play politics as they engage in group actions, strikes, and other manifestations. There are national political organizations for students who wish to join. There is a close relationship between students and faculty along party lines. In this way, a pupil assigned to memorize Dialogue 13 for pattern drill has also memorized an important feature of Spanish American culture. Few pupils fail to have their curiosity aroused by such material, and they seem to have little difficulty in retaining the information.

The answer to the supposed "anticultural" bias of the audio-lingual approach is that this cultural material is not incidental. The dialogues are planned from the first with the cultural aspect clearly in mind.

A set of cultural footnotes (e.g., *Modern Spanish*, second edition, p. 207, and our own Chapter 2, pp. 20–24) follows the dialogue, so that the cultural focuses need not be discussed in class, if the teacher chooses. The cultural "point" of the dialogue is still obvious. Should the teacher care to make a more pointed lesson of these notes, three or four minutes may be spent either during the situational presentation of the dialogue, at the end of the dialogue, or during the "check-up" on cultural matters.

The third step in the cultural presentation comes after the pupil has learned the dialogue. When the teacher conducts the check-up session to make sure that the dialogue has been memorized and understood, several questions concerning the cultural content of the dialogue should be included. The questions must, of course, be kept within the linguistic grasp of the student at the moment; yet they should be to the point and should help him to isolate the significant features of Latin-American culture contained in the dialogue. An occasional brief remark in English is also possible. Here, the well-informed teacher can make use of linguistic cues from the dialogue itself. The use of "formal" and "informal" address reveals a culturally significant view of Hispanic society — one worth mention from the outset. Forms of greetings, farewells, presentations, and the like are equally significant.

Organization is important. The mere mention of facts that happen to be related to a current activity is ineffective as a device for teaching culture. Cultural matter should form a specific body of information within which knowledge, attitude, and appreciation are incorporated. Here, again, the traditional textbook fails us. It either concentrates on one cultural feature to the detriment of all other values or is inconsistent in its cultural approach.

Many texts, both traditional and modern, present distorted views of Hispanic-American and Peninsular culture, focusing undue attention on "colorful" folkways which, in the urban centers, are regarded by native residents as quaint and which are, even from the urban native's point of view, as strange to him as to the American student learning Spanish. Industrialization, complex economic development, housing, transportation, public health, immigration, and education are far more serious preoccupations in Spain and Latin America today than the amorous nocturnal serenades, *tortilla*-and-*frijoles* meals, romantic gaucho life, and adobe villages which have for so long been the chief cultural concern of Spanish textbooks. Soccer, skiing, cockfighting, as well as horseback riding, tennis, and swimming are sports as important to most Spanish-speaking peoples as bullfighting. While it is true that a study of more complex social questions in the Spanish-speaking world cannot be undertaken during the four-year sequence in most secondary schools, it is urgent that those cultural focuses we do present be scrupulously accurate and representative.

The carefully planned audio-lingual text is as systematically organized in its treatment of culture as in its treatment of language. If it appears to devote comparatively fewer pages to cultural phenomena, it is only because at the beginning level, as we have said, primary emphasis is necessarily on the language skills.

During the first two years, it is possible to present cultural material in Spanish as a part of the regular program of language learning. But, as pupils develop, their own cultural interest (music, art, government, literature, science, etc.) transcends their linguistic facility, and a widening breach becomes evident between their real interests and their ability to learn about them and discuss them in Spanish.

We know that, as the student begins his study of Spanish, his interest in Spanish culture and civilization far transcends his ability to pursue them in Spanish. During the first year, because our emphasis remains necessarily on skill acquisition, we must draw our socio-cultural focuses from the language material itself. By the end of a year of language study, however, the student will begin to be able to pursue his cultural interests in Spanish, although not with the total ease which he will acquire much later on.

By the third and fourth years of language study, the pupils' linguistic competence gradually catches up with their cultural interests, making it possible to introduce significant doses of cultural material in Spanish in the classroom, laboratory, and homework program. Of course, we do not want to limit the pupils' field of inquiry, and yet, because the chief objective of the first two years is to teach communication skills, the best method of developing these skills may not always include a primary concentration on cultural content.

It is at this point that many teachers permit the use of English for outside readings on cultural topics. Such projects during the first two years are permissible only so long as we are always careful to devote class time first and foremost to audio-lingual drill. Probably, English-language cultural activities are best treated as outside projects, graded or not, with — at the very most — an occasional summary in class. If a summary can simply be in the form of a map, chart, or picture to be posted in class, so much the better. The pupils' cultural awareness will be enriched and the overall "Hispanic" look of the room itself will be enhanced at no cost of precious class time.

The map is a useful stimulus to such outside cultural activities at the beginning levels. Students can use desk outline maps or make their own. On them they can draw boundaries, outline countries where Spanish is the official language, show principal products of Spanish-speaking nations, or illustrate the geographical spread of ethnic groups. Such information is readily found in encyclopedias, geographies, and other books generally available in school libraries. Both the research and actual drawing may be done at home, scheduled so as not to interfere with dialogue memorization and other linguistic activities.

Celebration of holidays is another exercise which is popular and not too time-consuming. Still other activities include hunting for Spanish words or expressions used in newspapers, radio, television, books and magazines; gathering names of Spanish and Spanish-American foods, identifying them, finding when and where they are eaten; learning songs; collecting prints or pictures of famous paintings, statues, or buildings, and preparing brief descriptions in Spanish.

Howard Nostrand has suggested the following as valuable cultural experiences within the context of the language-learning sequence.[1]

1. Situation dialogues — controlled for elementary instruction, and candid for more advanced teaching, but all preferably on film. Existing materials will illustrate the kinds of situation that are worth presenting — between age mates, host and guest, neighbors, persons of unequal social status. Students need more guidance, however, in formulating what each situation illustrates of the foreign behavior patterns.

2. Programmed audio materials, designed for self-instruction, expounding aspects of the culture, social system, or history of a country.

3. Spoken descriptions of museum materials, such as paintings, handicrafts, model villages, to accompany pictures of the objects. Students can listen to the museum "acoustiguides" commentary in the language lab, looking meanwhile at a printed catalogue of the materials.

4. Literature taught in its relation to the culture and society. Recitations of poems, brief prose narratives, and monologues, accompanied by cultural commentary to be read by the students, or listened to in the language laboratory, or presented by the teacher in the class discussion. Recitations by contemporary authors of selections from their writings.

5. Songs significant of a way of life. Film can show how work songs, festival songs, etc., are used in the country; a booklet can present to the teacher or students the generalizations that confer significance upon the example.

6. Motion pictures as art form and social document. Margaret Mead suggests that students see half of a film and test their understanding of the foreign culture's art forms by guessing how the story will end. A check sheet of types of behavior patterns to look for, with some preliminary instruction, enables students to discover in a motion picture (or documentary film) a wealth of paralinguistic, kinesic, and social patterns which open up a new world for observation. [Please see pp. 162–163 for some general techniques for the use of film as a language learning experience.]

7. Filmed or taped interviews of social types significant in the country and excerpts from talks given by political and other leaders, could well be more extensively used at a more advanced stage of language learning when long works of literature cannot yet be read at a sufficiently rapid pace to become engaging.

---

[1] In the *Florida FL Reporter*, Vol. 3, No. 2 (January 1965), 2 and 18.

8. Testing understanding and the ability to communicate. The language laboratory can present, on film or tape, excerpts of such materials as have been suggested, calling for a response that will indicate the student's understanding and/or his ability to react acceptably. The learner's ability to follow an informal conversation with ease, for example, gives one indication of his acquaintance with the foreign way of life. His nearness to native proficiency in understanding discourse could be measured still more exactly by refinements such as the 'close procedure' in which words are blanked out, at regular or random intervals.

A certain amount of outside reading is implicit in the activities we have mentioned. Formal reading assignments, however, present a more complex problem. Extensive reading in English has no place in the Spanish language curriculum, yet it may become necessary for students to do *some* outside cultural reading in English. To make such reading a meaningful *linguistic* experience as well, it is necessary to insist that students summarize or dramatize in Spanish the content of what they read in English. At all events, it is best to avoid such English reading as much as possible. Music, art, and other cultural activities should be indulged in only when they do not take time from the audio-lingual practice, which is the heart of the first two years.

Some teachers have found that devoting the first five minutes of the hour to the singing of Spanish or Spanish-American songs "limbers up" the voice for intensive oral drill, relaxes the students, puts them in a more "Spanish" frame of mind, and is time well spent. Furthermore, teachers maintain that the effort of memorizing the lyrics has a beneficial linguistic effect as well. There can be no serious objection to such activities when the teacher finds that better language learning takes place because of them and when the time devoted to them is strictly limited.[2]

In most schools, teachers in charge of advanced courses have fulfilled this cultural need mostly through reading. In Chapter 7, we discussed the general position of reading in the audio-lingual approach. Now we shall discuss in more detail the things to be read and the goals to be set. Too often, we tend to think that cultural readings in the

---

[2] The full potential of the language laboratory as an adjunct to learning in advanced courses is only now being realized. Some insights into its use in the teaching of literature in the foreign language sequence may be gained by reading Jeanne Pleasants, "A Language Laboratory Lesson Based on a Literary Text," *The Language Laboratory and the Teaching of Literature* (New York: Columbia University, 1961), pp. 27–36.

advanced course must be literary. Actually, literature is only one sub-division of the total possible cultural content of our courses. The following general outline shows that a wide variety of cultural topics is suitable, so long as the works being read are written by native speakers, are carefully edited, and are accurate in what they say:

   I. The Hispanic World Today
      A. the Spanish language
      B. Spanish influences in the United States
      C. relations between Spanish America and the United States

  II. Area Information (Spain and Spanish America)
      A. geography
      B. topography
      C. ethnography
      D. products and trade

 III. Cultural Patterns (varying, of course, from country to country)
      A. family life
      B. dress and diet
      C. recreation
      D. music and the arts
      E. holidays and festivals
      F. religion
      G. customs
      H. occupations
      I. education
         etc.

  IV. History of the Hispanic World
      A. Spain
          1. Spain before the Romans
          2. Roman Spain
          3. Spain under the Moors
          4. the Reconquest (Inquisition, etc.)
          5. the discovery of America
          6. defeat of the Armada
          7. Bourbon Spain
          8. loss of the colonies
          9. Spanish-American War
         10. Civil War (1936–1939)
         11. present-day developments

B. Spanish America
   1. discovery and conquest
   2. settlements and missions
   3. colonial period
   4. the struggle for independence
   5. problems of nationhood
   6. the OAS (OEA)
   7. present-day developments

V. Contributions of the Hispanic World to Western Civilization
   A. literature
   B. music
   C. painting, sculpture, and architecture
   D. science and technology

To limit the pupils' cultural exposure to literature alone is actually to cheat him of the general overview of Hispanic culture we should like him to have. The audio-lingual experience has taught us that, as examples of the written language and of culture, a history book or a biography written by a native speaker is as valuable to the secondary school pupil as a novel. Thus, we are no longer limited to the literary reader in our search for adequate cultural reading material in the advanced courses. Instead of a synthetic novel written by a non-native or editions of short stories which have been cut and edited beyond recognition, we are free to choose for the Spanish V student a book on, say, South American geography written for Spanish-speaking students of roughly the same age in Latin America. When it comes time to choose a novel or a play to illustrate Spanish or Spanish-American literature, the pupils will be better prepared to appreciate its historical and cultural context than previously.

Now, let us consider a typical sequence of cultural topics. Of course, there may not be time to cover all the areas on our outline, even in a six-year sequence. How the cultural information is to be covered must be left to the discretion of the teachers and supervisors in the individual districts. We need not worry about occasional opposition that may be encountered, because some of the material is touched on in social studies classes. In the context of language learning, the material has a totally different effect: there is a special intimacy, insight, and understanding as a reward of the pupils' identification of themselves with the language of other peoples in the sympathetic atmosphere of the Spanish class.

Sections I, II, III, and IV of the outline given above are the most suitable for early presentation (in the third and fourth years of the six-year sequence or in the third year of the four-year sequence). Much of the basic factual information about these areas will have been presented already in the context of the dialogues in the first two years (as we already mentioned earlier in the chapter). The most appropriate text will vary, depending upon pupils' abilities and the courses of study in individual schools. For some, one or another of the recently published surveys of Spanish civilization will be satisfactory, or perhaps a reader made up of contemporary Spanish-American essays on today's problems. For others, books on these specific topics prepared for Spanish-American schoolchildren of the same age will be more useful. It is hoped that current research will soon produce a series of graded readers on these topics. Until it does, the teacher still must choose from a wide field.

Section V of the outline is best presented in the final year of the four-year sequence and in the last two years of the six-year sequence. Here occurs the desired correlation between audio-lingual experience (which has continued throughout the program) and the study of culture. The goal is the ability to converse fluently in Spanish with a native speaker on several important topics of contemporary life. And this final stage is the one in which the student is best equipped to read and appreciate a novel in all its social and historical contexts.

Some Suggested Uses for Films as Audio-Lingual Teaching Devices

Film types: A. Target-language newsreels
             B. Travelogues in target language
             C. Feature films in target language
             D. Videotapes of television programs in target language

I. For "intensive" practice with film types A and B.

First day — Show film through once.
Show film again; students follow with script in hand.

Second day — Do repetition drill of each segment of sound track.
Assign each student 30–60 seconds of sound track to memorize.

Third day — Show film again, without sound; students provide sound track from memory.
Assign creation of "original" narration for each sequence.

Fourth day — Show film again, without sound; students provide sound track from original narrations.
Show film through, with original sound track.

II. For "extensive" practice with film types C and D.

First day   "Preview" film. Summarize in target language its content and what students are to look for, e.g., story line, characters, gestures, special uses of language, etc.
Show film.

Second day   Show film again, stopping projector at predetermined points to ask target language questions based on preview points.
Assign written exercise on these points.

Third day   General classroom discussion of film in target language.
(Optional, in language lab: Present on tape actual moments of original sound track. Ask students to describe the action of the film at the point from which the sound track tape was taken.)

▶ EXERCISES

1. Discuss how the cultural focus is integrated into the various levels of audio-lingual language instruction.
2. Discuss how the "inductive" approach to culture is achieved in the beginning levels of instruction.
3. Which cultural features of Hispanic civilization should be emphasized in the language program?
4. How is it possible to avoid the traditional and erroneous equation of culture and literature in language instruction?
5. By which means can pupils' attention be drawn to the cultural content of the linguistic material of the language lesson without consuming valuable skill-learning time?
6. Discuss the best means of and materials for achieving a realistic and up-to-date view of Hispanic culture in the secondary school foreign language curriculum, both from the teacher's and pupils' viewpoints.
7. Discuss the most productive uses of audio-visual presentations in the teaching of culture. Tie these in wherever possible with concomitant language-teaching objectives.
8. Discuss how viewing a Spanish-language motion picture can be developed into a meaninful cultural and linguistic learning experience.

REFERENCE BOOKS AND ARTICLES

BROOKS, NELSON. *Culture and Language Instruction* (New York: Harcourt, Brace & World, 1966).

———. "Teaching Culture in the Foreign Language Classroom" (*Foreign Language Annals* I, 1968), 204–217.

BROWN, R. W. *et al.* "Developing Cultural Understanding Through Foreign Language Study" (*PMLA* LXVIII, 1953), 1196–1218.

"Culture in Language Learning," in *Reports of the Working Committees of the 1960 Northeast Conference on the Teaching of Foreign Languages.*

EATON, ESTHER and MARY HAYES. *Source Materials for Secondary School Teachers of Foreign Languages* (Washington, D.C.: USOE Bulletin OE–27001, 1966).

HOCKETT, CHARLES F. "Relationships Between Development of Language Skills and Cultural Attitudes" (*California Schools* XXXI, 1960), 112–116.

HOIJER, HARRY, ed. *Language and Culture* (Chicago: University of Chicago Press, 1954).

NOSTRAND, HOWARD L. "Describing and Teaching the Sociocultural Context of a Foreign Language and Literature," in Albert Valdman, ed., *Trends in Language Teaching* (New York: McGraw-Hill, 1965).

11

Planning the four- and six-year sequences

The solid foundation we lay in the beginning years through the audio-lingual approach may easily be undone by reverting to the familiar alternation between review grammars and readers during the following years. At one time, when enrollments in advanced courses were small and generally made up of especially interested students, the dangers of poorly coordinated classes were limited. Now that a steadily growing number of pupils are enrolling in advance courses, it has become important to consider the continuity within our advanced courses of the approach with which we began in the first years.

As we have mentioned in preceding chapters, the four- or six-year sequence constitutes a "total language program" in which the skills of hearing, speaking, reading, and writing are not only presented but perfected throughout the entire sequence. This means that however much the emphases may change from skill to skill in a given semester or year, no skill is ever absent from the program. Thus, the integrity of the total language program is never lost, although the percentage of time and attention devoted to one or another skill may vary.

Before we can sensibly proceed to a consideration of what kind of audio-lingual drill is most profitable in the advanced years and of how it can be integrated with the extensive cultural content of advanced courses, we must first consider the relative balance of time allotted to each phase of language instruction throughout the four- or six-year sequence.

Because the exact percentages of time devoted to each aspect of language instruction will vary according to the requirements of each school district, the following figures are intended merely to suggest relative percentages of time to be allotted to each skill. Cultural material, because its preparation most often involves reading and writing, is considered in the following diagrams to be a part of the reading and writing phases.

From the following diagrams, we can observe that although there is a steadily increasing or decreasing degree of emphasis placed upon each skill at a specific level, all four skills have an important place in the total program at any given level.

THE SIX-YEAR PROGRAM							
Instructional focus	*Year:*	*1*	*2*	*3*	*4*	*5*	*6*
1. Hearing ⎫ 2. Speaking ⎭		80%	63%	43%	37%	23%	17%
3. Reading		17%	23%	37%	43%	50%	50%
4. Writing		3%	14%	20%	20%	27%	33%

THE FOUR-YEAR PROGRAM					
Instructional focus	*Year:*	*1*	*2*	*3*	*4*
1. Hearing ⎫ 2. Speaking ⎭		63%	43%	30%	23%
3. Reading		23%	37%	50%	50%
4. Writing		14%	20%	20%	27%

We have already observed that at the beginning levels of language instruction, a wide variety of syntactic drills (cf. Chapter 5) can be employed to teach the student how to manipulate the structures that he first encountered in the pattern dialogue. The purpose was to drill, one by one, each of the new structures that the pupil met. By the end of the first two years, using scientifically designed materials and the audio-lingual approach, most pupils have met and learned to use the fundamental structures of the language. During the third year and beyond, however, the purpose of audio-lingual drill is to perfect the pupil's control of the structures he has already met, and to present and drill for the first time some of the less frequent structures in the language or optional constructions, such as the choice between clause or infinitive after *dejar* and *hacer*.

During the first two years, we presented the new forms to be studied in the pattern dialogue. The dialogue had to be carefully created to focus attention on the new patterns and to include a controlled quantity of new vocabulary, unusual verb forms, idioms, and the like. From the third year on, however, the pupil has a sufficient control of the basic constructions of the language to read standard prose and not to be so confused by the presence of new forms that he cannot make sense out of it. Many textbook writers hold, moreover, that the abandonment of the dialogue in favor of prose selections at the advanced level aids in achieving the transition to reading and provides for a variety of more "colorful" uses of the language than could be possible in a realistic and believable dialogue. For the purposes of audio-lingual drill at advanced levels, there is little significant difference between pattern dialogues and literary or other cultural readings as a presentation device; therefore, in the advanced courses, we generally make use of cultural reading material such as we discussed in Chapters 7 and 10, instead of a pattern dialogue. In the advanced course, the reading material is the "corpus" from which the pupil will expand his recognition and working vocabulary and in which he will observe new variations in structural usage. In this way, the very reading material which forms the central part of the advanced course acts, as did the pattern dialogue in the early years, to present in context the structures to be learned.

The syntactic drill patterns we discussed in Chapter 5 are just as useful for advanced drills as they are for elementary exercises and no new prototypes need be created to achieve the desired results.

Once it has been decided, for example, that in a given advanced class approximately twenty-five percent of total class time will be devoted to audio-lingual practice, the teacher faces four immediate problems:

1. How shall the 25% of class time be divided? One class per week? Fifteen minutes each day? One week per month? etc.
2. Shall audio-lingual practice be performed in class only, or can the laboratory be used? If so, should it be used during the class hour or as reinforcement in addition to the classroom drill?
3. How shall the *appropriate* material be drawn from the readings?
4. How can the most effective grammatical generalization be made after the drills are completed?

First, let us consider how best to divide class time. The 25% figure refers not only to an amount of classroom time but also to the same relative percentage of homework time. Thus, audio-lingual experiences in the fourth year of a four-year program should take up approximately one quarter of *all* time (classroom, laboratory, and homework) devoted to the course. Here we note again how the language laboratory remains a key instructional device even at the advanced level. Its use in the cultural, literary, and testing phases of the advanced program is perhaps the area in which the language laboratory is least understood. Because, at the advanced level, it is just as necessary as at the beginning level to drill new structures as soon after encountering them as possible, approximately one quarter of each class hour should be devoted to audio-lingual drill. The manner of presentation does not differ from the sample lesson formula presented in Chapter 2:[1] (1) present pattern, (2) drill pattern, (3) generalization. Because the end of an audio-lingual drill is reached only when fluent responses are received from *all* pupils, it may well be that no more than one structure can be satisfactorily drilled in a given class period. This need not be alarming, however, since pupils are supposed to have mastered the high-frequency structure and vocabulary in the first years, so that there is less urgency in the advanced courses about the number of structures to be drilled in a given class hour.

It would be unrealistic, however, to assume that all students in an advanced class have mastered the fundamental language structures presented in earlier courses. This is due in part to a lack of uniformity among districts, schools, and even individual teachers in the way in which given levels of the language sequence are taught, and in part to the different learning abilities and retention potentials of each student. Therefore, the teacher must not be surprised if students stumble over an advanced structure drill because of incomplete mastery of the fundamental drills on the same structure presented one or two semesters before. It often happens that a student has considerable difficulty with a lesson on the uses of the imperfect subjunctive because he did not completely master the lesson on the forms of the imperfect subjunctive in previous semesters. For this reason, many teachers index their copies of the first level materials by structural focus and then bring these first-level books to their third- and fourth-level classes. When a student, such as the one referred to above in the subjunctive problem, stumbles in his performance of a drill because of faulty recall of the earlier lesson, the teacher may send him to the laboratory for additional practice by assigning him the taped drill from the earlier lesson. If several students fail in the same drill for a similar reason, the earlier drill can be done on the spot before continuing.

Second, should audio-lingual drill at the advanced level be a classroom exercise only? No. As we have come to appreciate the value of audio-lingual drill beyond the first level class, we have discovered that the

---

[1] Cf. pp. 20–24.

language laboratory, too, has a significant place in advanced audio-lingual drill. Just as we use the laboratory for reinforcement in the fundamental classes, so should laboratory practice be required in advanced classes to reinforce and overlearn advanced patterns. Each pupil, of course, will have different time requirements for mastery of a given structure, so no average laboratory time figure will be equally applicable for all. Generally, at the advanced level, thirty minutes of laboratory drill for each fifteen minutes of audio-lingual practice in class will serve to reinforce the structures. Of course, where it is not possible to insist on daily sessions of thirty minutes each in the language laboratory, such drill time as is possible will have to suffice. Ideally, the library-style laboratory is the most advantageous for these purposes. In no case, however, should students be required to practice at home without an authentic Spanish model. Here, the tape loan program mentioned in Chapter 6 may help ease the load on the laboratory and permit pupils to do their reinforcement exercises at home with their own tape recorder. Of course, those advanced texts which have their structure drills on take-home tapes and records, provide an opportunity for such practice.

Third, how do we select advanced audio-lingual material? Some materials, such as *A-LM*, *Entender y Hablar*, *Spanish for Secondary Schools*, and others, now provide sequential audio-lingual instructional materials sufficient to cover the entire secondary-school language sequence. The teacher's manuals which accompany these texts describe in some detail how the advanced units are to be used. But many schools prefer texts which do not yet have follow-up units for a complete four-year sequence. Teachers in these schools are usually obliged to use a combination of readers and review grammars (in the main not audio-lingual in design) in the advanced semesters. The dangers inherent in the use of many such readers have already been commented on in Chapter 10. The reference or review grammar usually fails to carry the student much beyond the vocabulary and structure he was to have learned in the first level of audio-lingual instruction, provides little well-designed structure drill, and offers little opportunity for oral practice. If the teacher is to achieve results in an advanced class without the aid of sequential texts, then the following procedure may be helpful.

The teacher must first scan the reading material for the semester. The object of this scanning is to make a list of constructions which were not studied during the first two years. These constructions, then, will form the basis of the semester's audio-lingual drill. A quick comparison of the scanning list and the topical index of the textbook used during the first two years will quickly yield a final list of constructions which will be new to the advanced student and which will, consequently, be the forms to be drilled. The exact list of constructions will depend upon which book was used in the first two years and which is being used in the advanced course. Among the most frequently encountered new structures are: the more detailed use of the imperfect subjunctive; future perfect for probability in past time; reflexives of unplanned occurrences; collective nouns; use of *tener*, *haber*, and *estar* without complements; etc.

Once the list of such constructions is formulated, the work of creating pattern drills to teach them begins. Most of the better audio-lingual texts provide ready-made drills. In the case of some constructions, the teacher will have to formulate his own, in accordance with the principles outlined in Chapter 5.

Each day's agenda of structural drill will depend upon which constructions have appeared in that day's reading assignment. It is generally not difficult to maintain a balance in the number of structures to be drilled from day to day, if the teacher is careful to note which of the constructions reoccur in the readings and can be drilled at a later date, as well as which constructions can be drilled together, as we shall see below.

Fourth, the grammatical generalization. The problem here is less one of locating the "explanation" in a reference grammar than of presenting the generalization in a truly descriptive, rather than prescriptive or normative, way. This can be accomplished as long as we bear in mind that the purpose of the generalization is to describe to the student what he has been doing as he has performed the drills.

Examining a sample advanced drill may give us a clue as to what is expected. The use of the past perfectives (*hubo hecho* and *había hecho*) is a frequent problem in advanced readers, and is therefore a likely subject for advanced audio-lingual drill. If a suitable drill cannot be found already prepared in an audio-lingual textbook, one must be created. Most up-to-date reference grammars will tell us honestly that the past anterior (*hubo hecho*) is not distinguished from the pluperfect (*había hecho*) by most contemporary speakers of Spanish. Where a distinction is made, it is generally a question of style, and in daily speech, the use of the past anterior is considered pleonastic. For these reasons we would pass over an occurrence of the past anterior in a reader and not stop to drill its use. The pluperfect, however, seems to have gained considerable ground in standard usage, replacing the past anterior in everyday speech. To begin the drill, a brief review of the imperfect forms of *haber* will probably be necessary. Once, perhaps twice, around the room with a brief conjugation drill (person-number

substitution) should suffice. Taking our cue from the principal use of
the pluperfect itself, our drill should concentrate upon the contrast
between the pluperfect and the preterite to make clear the difference
in past time being referred to. Because of a close parallel with English,
most students will perceive the contrastive usage at once. (A short,
but effective drill is found in *Modern Spanish*, second edition, p. 321.)
If, in the same reader, occurrences of other perfectives (future perfect,
conditional perfect, etc.) are found, the teacher may find it advantageous
to drill them all at once, making use of the structural similarity as an
aid to learning. The drills in *Modern Spanish*, mentioned above, are
formulated on this principle. The generalization which follows such
drill should emphasize the familiar parts the students have already
learned. A comparison with the present perfect of both Spanish and
English should be helpful. The statement that the pluperfect tells "what
already had happened at a given past time" is usually all the explanation pupils will require.

Audio-lingual drill is not limited to these uses alone, however. If a
play is being read, many teachers have the roles acted out, once the content and structure of the acts are understood and drilled. Then, using
a form similar to the sample echo evaluation in Chapter 8, the pupils
are evaluated on their oral production. Classroom drill on their errors
then follows, along the lines we suggested in Chapter 4. Because many
of the best Spanish plays are recorded, many teachers select a play on
the basis of the availability of a good recording of it. Students are then
assigned to prepare the lessons on the play in the language laboratory
while listening to the recording.

Reading aloud from texts other than plays is also useful, although
less representative of the spoken language. In this way, the same
readings are used for cultural, structural, and phonological purposes,
resulting in a far more economical and profitable use of class time. If a
school has funds to acquire or personnel to create tapes of the readings
used in class, pupils may then be required to reinforce their classroom
exercises in pronunciation by using the tapes as models in the language
laboratory. Where a laboratory has adequate dubbing facilities and
personnel, the master tape of the reading selection can be redubbed
and broken into phrases for repetition by the pupils. Otherwise, pupils
may be taught to manipulate the pause control [2] on their laboratory
equipment and given a marked manuscript of the work to indicate
where they should stop the tape in order to repeat the phrase they have
just heard.

---

[2] Cf. Chapter 6.

Some teachers prefer to test pupils in the language laboratory for their understanding of what they have read. To do this, three or four passages (generally of 100 words each) are selected and approximately ten multiple-choice questions on each passage are devised. Pupils have before them only an answer sheet with letters or numbers corresponding to the various choices. They see neither the text of the passage nor the questions and answer choices. Through their earphones in the laboratory (or from a high-fidelity tape recorder in the classroom, if a laboratory is not available), the pupils hear the passage read twice, at normal speed. The questions are then read twice, each time followed by the answer choices. Through this approach to testing for comprehension, many teachers feel that the pupil has not only profited from the reading material itself but also has gained more auditory proficiency. Of course, there are many variations on this activity. Some teachers prefer to allow students to choose from written questions and answers after they have heard the passage. Others present the passage and questions orally but permit pupils to choose from among written answers. There are disadvantages, however, in these variations, and there is some question as to their validity as testing procedures. Asking the student to master the content of a passage presented orally but to respond to the written language for his test questions on the passage is an unsound and confusing mixture of skills. Oral comprehension is best tested by having the students respond, either orally or in writing, to an *oral* stimulus. We are, of course, in no way limited to the multiple-choice answer here. Almost any of the comprehension tests mentioned in Chapters 7 and 8 are adaptable for this activity and good results have been obtained in experiments with them.

Now that we have an idea of what kinds of advanced audio-lingual experiences are possible, we can begin to formulate a broad outline for the six- and four-year sequences. In the six-year sequence, the audio-lingual phase (observing the approximate time distribution discussed at the beginning of this chapter) in grades 7 and 8 consists of the memorization of pattern dialogues; oral drill on pronunciation and structure; and an admixture of simple poems, songs, and recitations to stimulate interest and participation. The reading phase consists of learning to read the dialogues which have been memorized and of recombination narratives based on the vocabulary and structure already learned audio-lingually from the dialogues. In the final semester of the eighth grade, depending upon the general progress of the class, reading material not previously presented in class may be used, in small quantities. During both these years, all writing activity is guided. It begins by having pupils learn to write, both from memory and from dictation, the material they have already drilled audio-lingually in class. During the final semester of the eighth grade, however, simple transformations of audio-lingual material may be given. Pupils may be asked, during this final semester, to write out brief answers to dialogue questions which have already been drilled audio-lingually and read. The New York State manual [3] suggests that vocabulary building exercises may be included, in small doses, within this writing phase, through labelling familiar objects and making picture dictionaries. Again, the inherent danger of wasting too much class time on such activities militates against making more than very occasional use of them. At this stage, the cultural content must be developed almost exclusively through the dialogues. Some of the most elementary cultural activities suggested in Chapter 10 may be employed only if the class has demonstrated its proficiency in the other skills and, of course, must be limited to a small percentage of the total course time.

In grades 9 and 10, audio-lingual experiences remain the prime objective. All structures are presented and drilled audio-lingually. Vocabulary and idioms are also presented and drilled orally. Because a general increase in reading activity begins in this phase, a gradual coordination of reading experiences and audio-lingual practice is begun, as suggested earlier in this chapter. In the tenth grade, oral reporting on topics from the readings, followed by pronunciation drill, is a valuable activity. During this period, extensive reading is introduced and then expanded. It has been found that, as mentioned in Chapters 7 and 10, the reading experience is much more profitable when a wide variety of printed forms (literary works, geography and history books, and newspapers and periodicals) is used as the basis for the selection of reading materials. The writing phase continues to represent what pupils can already say and read. As the audio-lingual and reading activities increase, so does the scope of the writing phase. Dictations, recombinations of already learned patterns, answers to questions, writing of all drill patterns, and, if progress is satisfactory, some letter writing on familiar topics are used. (Cf. Chapter 7.)

The current nationwide trend toward initiating six-year foreign language instruction sequences beginning in the seventh grade, and sometimes below, has created serious problems in articulation. In many school districts in which FLES programs are in operation, for example, no provisions exist for advanced placement at the secondary-school level, and the pupils are forced to begin their studies anew. Thus, the

---

[3] *Spanish for Secondary Schools* (Albany: New York State Department of Education, 1961).

advantage they have gained through early foreign language study and much of the motivation for doing so are minimized by the need to return to the beginning on entering the secondary school. In other districts, in which FLES programs do not exist or are not meant to be the first phase of an articulated continuing program of foreign language study, it is often possible to begin foreign language study in the seventh grade. However, pupils in this type of program, like their FLES counterparts, find that upon transferring from the intermediate or junior high school into the high school (usually at the ninth or tenth grade levels), there is either no continuing course appropriate to their level of proficency or, where such courses do exist, placement is achieved in virtually random fashion. Moreover, because the format of foreign language instruction in the intermediate school often differs considerably from that in the high school (e.g., three sessions of twenty-five minutes each per week in some intermediate schools as opposed to five sessions of fifty-five minutes per week in the high school), it is rare that a "complete" course of study equal to an entire "level" of foreign language instruction before entering the high school program is accomplished.

To resolve these difficulties, several solutions have been proposed. First, some high schools simply force entrants with intermediate school exposure to foreign language instruction to start over again. Second, they may advance these students to the second "level," even when they may not be fully prepared for it. In part, these procedures are dictated by the absence of physical and financial resources sufficient to administer a complete battery of placement examinations in foreign languages at the high school for each incoming student. And even if some schools had the required personnel and facilities, nationally normed placement exams for students with only one or two years of intermediate school language study are not available. Moreover, the divergent teaching schedules between intermediate school and high school foreign language programs which we have mentioned often force the intermediate school curriculum planners to select different materials than those which are in use in the high school.

In view of these problems, it is no wonder that articulation is difficult. And because it is so, the placement of intermediate school language students in high school language programs often becomes a matter of guesswork, in which the intermediate school language teacher attempts to "predict" the success of the language student in high school.

The system of vertical articulation described below is an attempt at one possible solution to the articulation problem. It has obvious limitations, principal among which is that it is designed for a program of foreign language study beginning in the seventh grade. It is hoped, however, that, at least in principle, it can be modified for use by districts with an earlier or later initiation point.

These are the basic assumptions of the program outlined below: first, the seventh- and eighth-grade levels meet for an average of 58 contact hours per academic year; the ninth through twelfth grade levels meet for an average of 174 contact hours per academic year. The difference is usually attributable to intermediate school scheduling in which classes meet for shorter periods of instruction, often on a 3-day-per-week plan. Second, it is assumed that the same set of sequenced instructional materials is used throughout the program. In the case of this program, it happens that the materials used are *A-LM Spanish*. No endorsement of this particular set of materials is implied or intended. Any sequential audio-lingual materials would theoretically serve the purpose, and the choice of specific materials must remain with each district, although because most modern foreign language teaching materials are designed to present approximately the same amounts of structure and vocabulary over a particular sequence of units, differences between any pair of teaching texts usually are found in the comparative efficiency and thoroughness of their methodological format.

COURSE I: All students are eligible to enter Course I. In it, three units are taught in a full 4-skill presentation. Each unit is done audio-lingually in a horizontal presentation, i.e., first half of dialogue followed by all pertinent drills; second half of dialogue followed by all pertinent drills; and finally, the recombination material. The emphasis is on a high criterion of performance. Each segment of these three units is done with great care, not advancing to the next until the present one is done to perfection.

In the printed materials, the general organization of these initial three units follows the outline on pp. 20–24. Our outline, however, referred to a full four-skill presentation of each of these units, so, from the very beginning, a reading and writing sequence is built in. After a unit has been done audio-lingually, we return to the beginning of the same unit in order to re-do it, this time with emphasis on the reading and writing skills:

  I. Brief explanation of the problem of interference.
   A. Nature of interference
   B. Insistence on a "standard" pronunciation
 II. The target-language alphabet
III. Implications of reading
   A. Pronouncing words and phrases aloud in response to the stimulus of the printed words

B. Following printed sequence rapidly for comprehension with the eye scanning whole groups of words at a time

C. "Intensive" reading

IV. Mass association practice based on dialogue

V. Interference drill

VI. Graphic minimal pairs (based on phonetic drill)

VII. Graphic representations of selected sound contrasts

VIII. Reading

IX. Imitative writing

X. Dictation

At the end of Course I, a four-skill proficiency test is given, in which each skill is tested separately. The "fluency" factor is tested by a series of four visual stimuli, analogous to the situations presented in the basic dialogues for the three units involved. Students are asked to "talk about" the first two for one minute each on tape. Students are asked to "write about" the second two for three minutes each on paper. The results of the individual sections of the test are correlated in approximately equal parts. The upper half automatically advances to Course I A, while the lower half advances to Course I B. No one is eliminated from the program at this point, except in cases where the counselling staff feels it advisable for nonlinguistic reasons.

Course I A: Because the placement procedure at the end of Course I guarantees a fairly uniform high level of proficiency, students in Course I A will be expected to cover units 4 through 11, in a full 4-skill presentation. Again, the printed materials generally adhere to the internal structure presented on pp. 20–24, with the following two additions:

I. Readings

A. In written form

B. On tape in the laboratory to check auditory comprehension

II. Response drills based on readings

A. In written form for orthographic practice

B. In the laboratory and in class for oral practice

In order to achieve the full 4-skill presentation required, the following supplementary steps are added. Again, after completing each unit audio-lingually, we return to the beginning of the unit and re-do it with emphasis on the reading and writing skills:

I. Mass association practice

II. Interference drill

III. Graphic minimal pairs

IV. Graphic representation of selected sound contrasts

    V. Reading
   VI. Imitative writing
  VII. Dictation
 VIII. Written answers
       A. Oral stimuli
       B. Printed stimuli
          1. Answer
          2. Rejoinder
   IX. Rewriting — first phase
       A. Dialogue to narrative
       B. Narrative to dialogue
    X. Written responses to pattern drill stimuli
   XI. Rewriting — second phase
       A. Transformation
          1. Tense/aspect
          2. Person
       B. Summary

At the end of the course, a full 4-skill test will be given, plus a "fluency" test paralleling the one given at the end of Course I but appropriate to the units taught. The test results are correlated with performance, and the pupils are ranked. The upper two-thirds of the students advance to Course II AA, while the lower one-third advances to Course II A.

COURSE I B: As in the case of Course I A, the placement procedures followed at the conclusion of Course I guarantee a high degree of uniformity in proficiency among students in Course I B. These students will be expected to complete units 4–7 in a full 4-skill presentation. The printed materials for these units generally follow the format as outlined on pages 20–24. They are to be supplemented with the reading and writing procedures outlined on pages 109ff. At the end of the course, a full 4-skill test, including a "fluency" factor is to be given. The test results are correlated with classroom performance and the pupils are ranked. The upper third will advance to Course II A, while the lower two-thirds will advance to Course II B.

COURSE II AA: Because only the highest two-thirds of those students completing Course I A are admitted, Course II AA can easily accomplish the nine rather substantial units prescribed. The general outline of the units under study follows the format presented on pages 24 and 25. The same general testing format as above, but with stronger emphasis on the reading and writing skills, is used for the final evaluative examination. After correlating the test results with classroom performance, the pupils are ranked; the upper half advances to Course IV in the now regular sequence. The lower half advances to Course III A.

Courses II A and III A: Composed of students from the lower third of Course I A and of the upper third of Course I B, this course will progress more deliberately than Course II AA and will emphasize the transition from the predominant dosage of audio-lingual skills to the more equal balance of all four language skills as characterized by the composition of the materials themselves. As before, the results of the final evaluative examination are to be correlated with classroom performance and a ranking achieved. All students, however, with passing grades will advance to Course III A, which will bring students through Unit 20. At the end of Course III A, the upper half is advanced to Course IV in the regular sequence, while the lower half is terminated.

Courses II B and III B: The emphasis in these courses is upon the reading and writing skills, without losing sight of the continuing audio-lingual skill practice. The pace is quite moderate, permitting the slower student to receive the greater attention he requires. The lower half is terminated at the end of Course II B, while the upper half progresses through Course III B, at the end of which the upper half progresses to Course III A, and the lower half is terminated.

This system, with modifications appropriate to the individual districts in which it may be operative, provides adequately for the major variations in language learning proficiency while at the same time making possible the encouragement of the weakest students to seek courses in other areas after having had a *fair* chance to achieve criterion performance in a group of *appropriately* competitive talent.

In grades 11 and 12, the audio-lingual phase is integrated with all course activities along the lines discussed earlier in this chapter. The reading phase is essentially extensive and produces best results when reading selections are chosen from a wide variety of printed sources. Toward the end of the twelfth grade, however, intensive reading of literary works in different forms is suggested. The authors selected should provide the student with material for a minimum understanding of an epoch in Hispanic literary development. Attention may be paid to style, historical context, etc. Audio-lingual activity should accompany the reading program throughout. The writing phase is expanded to include both controlled and free composition (cf. Chapter 7). Toward the end of the twelfth grade, summarizing and paraphrasing of lectures, tapes, and books should be encouraged, and note-taking in Spanish practiced.

ARTICULATED SEQUENCE

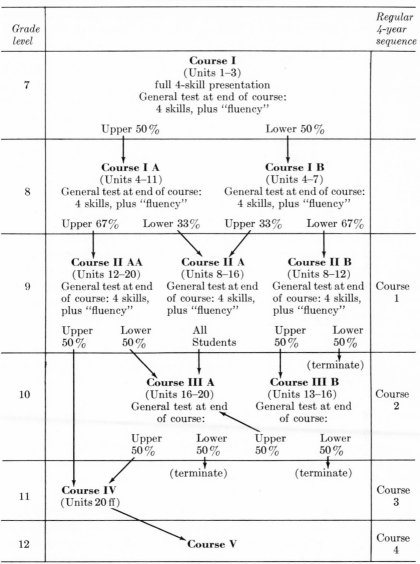

Grade level		Regular 4-year sequence
7	**Course I** (Units 1–3) full 4-skill presentation General test at end of course: 4 skills, plus "fluency" — Upper 50% Lower 50%	
8	**Course I A** (Units 4–11) General test at end of course: 4 skills, plus "fluency" — Upper 67% Lower 33% **Course I B** (Units 4–7) General test at end of course: 4 skills, plus "fluency" — Upper 33% Lower 67%	
9	**Course II AA** (Units 12–20) General test at end of course: 4 skills, plus "fluency" — Upper 50% Lower 50% **Course II A** (Units 8–16) General test at end of course: 4 skills, plus "fluency" — All Students **Course II B** (Units 8–12) General test at end of course: 4 skills, plus "fluency" — Upper 50% Lower 50%	Course 1
10	(terminate) **Course III A** (Units 16–20) General test at end of course: — Upper 50% Lower 50% **Course III B** (Units 13–16) General test at end of course: — Upper 50% Lower 50%	Course 2
11	**Course IV** (Units 20 ff) (terminate) (terminate)	Course 3
12	**Course V**	Course 4

Because many school districts have evolved excellent programs of instruction in Spanish in the elementary schools, some special thought must be given to the sequences in the secondary schools of these districts. While it is not our intent to discuss the FLES programs, the number of students entering the secondary schools with previous exposure to Spanish will steadily grow with the increased nationwide emphasis on FLES. This will necessitate a modification of the proposed six- or four-year sequence discussed here, since what is proposed for eighth grade may be accomplished in the seventh, and so on. The obvious result is the opportunity to effect a truly advanced course in civilization and culture in the twelfth grade in which a wide variety of materials, historical, literary, and artistic may be used for reading and discussion and supplemented with a generous amount of films, reports, etc. Those schools which are located in the area of a college or university and are fortunate enough to have a television hook-up with the college may well be able to allow the students to observe the lectures of the college class in civilization and culture, via T.V., for three days of the week, keeping the remaining two days for discussion and other activities in the high school classroom. In some cases the high school seniors may be allowed to attend the classes at the college during this year and while they are receiving credit for the course as part of their high school career, they are also profiting by the fact that this credit may be used for an Advanced Placement program when they enter college.

It cannot be overemphasized that in those districts having a good program of foreign language instruction in the elementary and junior high schools, it is very necessary and profitable for the secondary teachers to hold periodic meetings with the teachers in the lower schools for purposes of articulation in order to assure the smooth transition of the students progressing through the various stages of the sequence, to guard against waste of effort on part of the teachers at various levels in the program, and to assure the student the maximum of achievement in the given number of years in the sequence.

The same general lines of development are observed in the four-year sequence: grade 9 corresponds roughly to the activities of grades 7 and 8 in the six-year sequence; grade 10 corresponds roughly to grades 9 and 10 in the six-year sequence; grades 11 and 12 correspond generally to their counterparts in the six-year sequence. This implies that the intensity and single-mindedness of objectives in the first two years of the four-year sequence must be greater than in the longer program. This is partly mitigated by the greater maturity of the ninth-grade student who may be more ready to accept an intensive program than is his seventh-grade counterpart.

A recent development in some progressive districts has been programs tailored to the abilities and motivations of the students, eliminating the current system of semester courses with a passing grade in first semester guaranteeing promotion to the second semester, etc. In its place, the courses are offered by *level*. Regardless of the grade received in Level I, admission to Level II depends on a certain minimum score on a diagnostic examination (preferably the MLA tests or some such instrument of measurement which has national norms and/or norms established in the local situation). This means, of course, that the more gifted student could be allowed to progress to Level II within the same semester or year, while the slow learner may be required to take one extra semester to finish the prescribed work before passing the test required for promotion.

Eventually, and if the relatively complex system of articulation described above cannot be implemented, one could provide a two-semester course for slow learners doing one semester's regular work, and a one-semester course for fast learners doing two semesters' work. The following chart suggests a pattern which might be followed in programs which allow some flexibility of this type.

	Traditional Pattern; Average Learners	*Fast Learners*	*Slow Learners*
1st Year:	Level I	Level I Level II	Level I
2nd Year:	Level II	Level III	Level I
3rd Year:	Level III	Level IV	Level II
4th Year:	Level IV	Advanced civilization/culture course	Level II
	Summary: 8 semesters with 4 units of credit	*Summary:* 8 semesters with 4 units of credit plus 1 year of college credit (Advanced Placement)	*Summary:* 8 semesters with 2 units of credit

Such a program must, of course, have the provision that any student may move in either direction to join another group at the level for which he is prepared after successfully completing the required test. A slower learner may be so motivated as to join the average group, or the average student may move up to the pace of the fast learner and thereby be able to work toward the Advanced Placement course.

The division into grades which we have observed in our discussion corresponds to the standard semester divisions in most school systems.

It would be most satisfactory, of course, to permit pupils to progress to the succeeding phase just as soon as they demonstrate genuine proficiency. Some schools have used the MLA proficiency test in Spanish skills to determine whether or not pupils are ready to be advanced by skipping a semester. This can be only partly satisfactory, however, since the end of the semester in a given school system may not totally coincide with the acquisition of proficiency in a given skill sufficient to warrant omission of the following semester.

▶ EXERCISES

1. The chart presented in this chapter which suggests percentages of time to be devoted to various skills shows a marked decrease from 80% to 17% between the first and sixth years in the emphasis on hearing and speaking. Discuss this apparent "abandonment" of the teaching of oral skills as the sequence progresses.
2. What is the comparative value of using, in the advanced courses, drills from the lower level courses as opposed to new drills on materials learned in previous semesters?
3. The opponents of the audio-lingual approach are strong in their feeling that the audio-lingual procedures cannot be maintained beyond the first, or possibly the second, year. How can you refute this?
4. Would it be possible and plausible to introduce free composition, prepared speeches, etc. earlier than the last year of a four-year sequence? Why?
5. What is the place of readings, reports, films, etc. *in English* in a course devoted to Hispanic civilization and culture in the final year of a six-year sequence?
6. Discuss the possibility of initiating and administering programs for slow and fast learners at your school, as suggested in this chapter.
7. A twelfth-grade Spanish class is assigned a novel and a play as required textbooks. In addition, one hour each week is devoted to reports of current events in Spanish. Songs are occasionally learned, and time is taken for the celebration of the Spanish holidays. The homework assignments consist of "understanding ten pages of the texts." In class, the teacher double-checks the assignment by asking the pupils questions about the content and having them translate passages. Comment on the positive and negative aspects of this approach, mention the probable results of this approach on the various phases of pupils' proficiency in linguistic skills and cultural awareness, and suggest modifications for the expansion of the course to cover all the necessary skills.

REFERENCE BOOKS AND ARTICLES

Spanish for Secondary Schools (Albany: Bureau of Secondary Curriculum Development, New York State Education Department, 1961).

Curricular Change in the Foreign Languages, 1963 Colloquium on Curricular Change (Princeton: College Entrance Examination Board, 1963).

Foreign Languages: Grades 7–12, Curriculum Bulletin Series V (Hartford: State of Connecticut Advisory Committee on Foreign Language Instruction, 1958).

Advanced Placement Program: Course Description (Princeton: College Entrance Examination Board, 1964).

GIDUZ, H. "What Do the Colleges Expect of the Entering Student in Foreign Languages?" (*Modern Language Journal* XLII, 1953), 174–176.

PALMER, L. R. "The Module — A New Mode for Gaining Flexibility" (*Minnesota Foreign Language Bulletin* VII, 1967), 1–6.

SACKS, NORMAN. "The Art of the Spanish Textbook, 1917–1967" (*Hispania* L, 1967), 875–887.

12

Inferring meaning and vocabulary building

Many times throughout preceding chapters, it has been repeated that language learning activities which present forms for "memorization" out of context are contrary to the principles of language pedagogy as we have been discussing them. Admittedly, there is a point beyond which lack of time makes it impractical to present new vocabulary items in pattern dialogue and to drill them, one by one, in contextual structure drills until they become habitual, regardless of the obvious advantages. For this reason, we must look briefly at techniques for vocabulary building by inferring meanings.

Our concern throughout the book, except for our remarks concerning reading and culture, has been oriented toward the development of the pupil's active linguistic abilities, i.e., his ability to reproduce and recombine linguistic patterns according to the structure of the language. We have discussed teaching him to express himself intelligibly, albeit simply, in spoken and written form. In this chapter, we shall turn our attention to what is an essentially passive linguistic experience: grasping meaning, even when some element is unknown. We have discussed extensive reading, of course, where the pupil is expected to come across words and structures he does not know and which he must look up and learn. Here, we shall consider building the pupil's intuition about the target language that will serve him when it is not convenient to look up items.

Some methodologists suggest that this is a "self-solving" problem in that, as their cultural interests grow, pupils will repeat the fundamental vocabulary relating to their interests so often that they will add these words to their automatic active vocabularies without further drill. Any other terms must be looked up in the dictionary. After all, they maintain, no one ever fully outgrows his need for the dictionary. Others disagree. The latter do not deny that everyone who is not a native speaker will have to refer to the dictionary, and perhaps frequently. They do maintain, however, that pupils can be shown a systematic way in which to increase their passive (recognition) vocabulary and, at the same time, to increase their linguistic intuition — a prime factor in fluency.

Classroom teachers have not ignored the problem. Since most pupils who complete the four- or six-year sequences do so in order to gain college admission, some way must be found to expand vocabulary if they are to succeed in their courses in culture and civilization, literature, and advanced language structure. Thus, most teachers recognize the need for some kind of vocabulary-building activity, especially in the final year of high school, but are handicapped by a lack of prepared materials. Yet this is such an important activity that we cannot afford to overlook it or leave it to the pupil to do on his own.

We can begin most easily by recognizing that vocabulary building can be systematized into a series of carefully constructed drills, not unlike those we have discussed, in order to achieve specific results. The goal of this sort of classroom drill is to teach the pupil what is involved in applying all he knows about the Spanish language and his own life experiences to guessing the meaning of words by inferring from context. But is this not something the pupil has been doing, perhaps unconsciously, since he began his language studies? Of course it is, but on a hit-or-miss basis.

We can say, of course, that the memorization of each pattern dialogue from the very first lesson was an exercise in vocabulary building. The introduction of a systematic effort to increase vocabulary, however, belongs to the reading phase discussed in Chapter 7. Two of the most popular vocabulary-building techniques based on readings have been used by most teachers from the beginning semester. First, we have long taught students to associate words with specific objects. The idea, here, is to fix the "vision" of the object firmly in the pupil's mind in such a way that the thought of it calls up its Spanish name, without reference to English. The obvious limitations of this technique — above all, its comparative uselessness in teaching forms other than substantives — usually prevent its continued use as an intensive drill device in the advanced years. Second, we have also made use of cognates by calling our pupils' attention to the many exact and near cognates in English and Spanish.[1] This activity is generally a valuable one, but caution must be exercised to warn pupils about what the French call *faux amis*, that is, apparent cognates which differ in meaning from language to language, such as English *sensible*, meaning having, using, or showing good sense, as opposed to Spanish *sensible*, with the idea of sensitive.[2]

But to stop here, as many teachers have felt they must for lack of materials, is wrong. First, there are many limits to these coganate and cognate-type exercises. Most easily recognizable cognates are not words for which the student is apt to have much use — they tend to be infrequent and technical or scientific. Furthermore, pupils tend to think of cognates as hispanicized English words and revert to thinking in English phonological and structural terms when they try to learn these new items. Thus, while starting off with cognates frequently instills an air of confidence in the pupil (for he apparently recognizes a thousand or so Spanish forms immediately, through his knowledge of English), his increased fluency and ease of comprehension will still depend rather upon his ability to deal with Spanish on its own terms, inferring the meaning of the Spanish form from the context of the Spanish phrase itself, without regard for possible similarities to English. We have all heard our students pronounce *nacional* as /našonál/, *tradición* as /tradišón/, or *animal* as /ænimál/.

As pupils advance we carry our exercises one step further by illustrating the great number of Spanish and English forms which differ from one another by suffix or prefix. This process is known as derivation, and most modern textbooks make some attempt at providing systematic exercises in derivation, although none really carries the study as far as might be desired.

Derivation is the name given to the grammatical process of composing new forms with new meanings by the addition of prefixes or suffixes to already existing root forms, such as in *atomic* from *atom*, *hardness* from *hard*. We can rapidly increase both the active and passive vocabularies by teaching the pupil to recognize the meanings of the various

---

[1] Dwight L. Bolinger. "1464 Identical Cognates in Spanish and English" *Hispania* XXXI (1948), pp. 271–279.

[2] Two useful studies for pointing up the extent of Spanish and English vocabulary similarities are: Rodríguez Bou, Ismael *et al.*, *A Study of the Parallelism of English and Spanish Vocabularies* (Río Piedras: Superior Educational Council of Puerto Rico, University of Puerto Rico, 1950); Marshall E. Nunn and Herbert A. Van Scoy, *Glossary of Related Spanish-English Words*, University of Alabama Studies, Number 5 (Alabama: University of Alabama Press, 1949).

derivational suffixes and prefixes. Here, of course, we must assume that the pupil already controls the root forms.

But many teachers feel that this emphasis on known roots or stems restricts their early derivation lessons to known vocabulary only. In later lessons, they drop the matter and never take it up again to meet the pupil's expanded vocabulary. This is really uneconomical, since the more expansive the pupil's vocabulary, the greater the number of root forms he will recognize.

Most audio-lingual texts include exercises on derivation. Below are examples taken from *Modern Spanish* (second edition, pp. 375ff).[3] Naturally, the unit in the text contains more extensive drills and an appropriate structure generalization at the end of the lesson which is not included in the following excerpt:

Verb	Noun
cooperar	cooperación
organizar	organización
mejorar	mejoramiento
sentir	sentimiento
ganar	ganancia
importar	importancia

The suffixes **-ción, -miento,** and **-ncia** are used to derive nouns from verbs.

Adjective	Noun
enfermo	enfermedad
seguro	seguridad

The suffix **-dad** is used to derive nouns from adjectives.

Noun	Adjective
nación	nacional
centro	central

The suffix **-al** is used to derive adjectives from nouns.

Affirmative	Negative
orden	desorden
componer	descomponer
ventaja	desventaja
necessario	innecesario
posible	imposible

The prefixes **des-, in-,** and **im-** reverse the meaning of a word.

The following are selected drills (also from *Modern Spanish,* 2nd ed.)[4] on the derivations presented above, in which the students are instructed to substitute the items listed for the word emphasized:

1. Del verbo **casar** viene el sustantivo **casamiento.**
   (pensar, llamar, mandar, acompañar, levantar, mejorar).
2. Del verbo **imaginar** viene el sustantivo **imaginación.**
   (exagerar, terminar, instalar, organizar, cooperar, participar,

---

[3] *Op. cit.*
[4] *Loc. cit.*

formar, invitar, felicitar, importar, presentar, eliminar, celebrar, investigar, significar).

3. Del adjetivo **relativo** viene el sustantivo **relatividad.**
   (sincero, oportuno, tranquilo, nervioso, bárbaro, seguro).

4. Del verbo **ganar** viene el sustantivo **ganancia.**
   (importancia, creencia, sugerencia, existencia, insistencia, preferencia).

5. Lo que es de la **profesión** se llama **profesional.**
   (nación, educación, materia, policía, presidencia, fruta, idea, medicina, secretaria, persona, semana).

6. Lo contrario de **orden** es **desorden.**
   (acuerdo, honor, nivel, unión, ventaja, apego, empleo).

7. Lo contrario de **dependiente** es **independiente.**
   (directo, exacto, necesario, perfecto, personal, posible, puntual, tranquilo).

Yet neither of these two activities of cognates and derivation begins to encompass the total scope of inferring meaning from contextual situations. For this reason, it is necessary to devise ways in which to duplicate as closely as possible in the target language the means by which the native speaker expands his own understanding. The best way in which to start the pupil on this is to show him how accurately and instinctively he does it in English. This can be done by selecting a stretch of English prose with a considerable number of technical or dialectal terms, or by inventing a stretch of standard prose and adding words of your own invention at frequent intervals. Examples of such invented phrases are, "Give me a *fryx* to sweep the room with" or "Give me a broom to *plyod* the room." The pupils are then asked to guess the meaning of the unknown words indicated. If they cannot find an exact equivalent, then they may give a brief definition or description of the term. They must be cautioned, however, to replace given grammatical forms with forms of the same class, i.e., a verbal expression for a verbal expression, an adjective for an adjective, etc. Most pupils will do surprisingly well from the very first. Of course, there will be terms which will be impossible to guess because of inconclusive contextual clues, but this should not be cause for discouragement.

Despite the high percentage of correct guessing, most pupils do not know by what process they inferred the correct meanings. The purpose of the exercise is to introduce them to some of the more frequent clues to meaning and how to spot them.

We know that, in most cases, word meanings are guessed correctly because the phrase in which they are framed serves to define them in some way. Returning to the example, "Give me a *fryx* to sweep the room with," the reader infers that a *fryx* must be something used to sweep with, hence a broom or something similar to a broom. Along these same lines, some of the unknown forms are so closely associated with the surrounding context that their meaning could easily be inferred even if they were omitted entirely, e.g., "We heard the rain _____ on the roof." In this phrase, the reader will almost unerringly choose the term "patter" or a close synonym, since the fundamental meaning is almost predetermined by the surrounding context. Thus, if the same phrase appeared as, "We heard the rain *kadder* on the roof," we should expect a similar degree of intuitive correctness in the guessed meaning.

The next step involves phrases containing forms which can be derived by deduction from relationships implied within the phrases. In these cases, the pupils infer the meanings by associating the phrases with their own life-experience of "how things act." In a phrase of the type, "He *kroded* the fire with a bucket of sand," the pupil can generally rightly infer that *kroded* must mean something like "put out" or "doused," since he knows from his own experiences that a bucket of sand thrown on a fire extinguishes it.

The pupils rapidly become aware that their guesses can be only approximate. Some of the more advanced pupils feel "cheated" because they have not looked up a "precise dictionary definition." They must be reminded that the inference of the general idea of what is being said is frequently more helpful than a precise definition, and, of course, that the whole idea of the exercise is to learn to understand what is being said or read "on the spot." Of course, the simple inference of general meaning is admittedly insufficient when dealing with scientific literature or conversation which must be understood exactly. For purposes of general conversation, however, it is sometimes of no help at all to know the exact meaning of a word. In the phrase, "I *zorred* the furniture with a cloth," we cannot be sure if the meaning of *zorred* is *cleaned, wiped, dusted, polished,* or something synonymous; but it is relatively certain that, if the student infers the idea of "cleaning," further refinements will add significantly to his understanding only if it is important to distinguish among various types of cleaning, e.g., if one were giving specific instructions to a maid. In the phrase, "The wheat was no good this year, for it *ackerspired* and sprouted in the ear, it being a very wet season," Seibert and Crocker call attention to the Welsh term *ackerspire.*

From the sentence we gather that when the wheat "ackerspires" it is no good, and that this condition is caused by too much rain; but unless we know . . . what effect an excess of rain has on wheat we will not know exactly the meaning of . . . "ackerspire," even should we find its technical translation in a dictionary.[5]

The student must content himself, even with the help of a dictionary, with knowing that when wheat *ackerspires*, it is spoiled in some way. Thus, these exercises provide the student with techniques and tools useful to him even when he does have access to reference books.

Not infrequently, the juxtaposition of synonyms or antonyms in a written phrase gives a clue as to the meaning of a form. In a phrase of the type, "He stood their *brasted*, at a loss for words one might say," the pupil may assume that *brasted* and "at a loss for words" describe approximately the same attitude. In phrases of the type, "Though the leaves were still green then, soon they would be *snig*," *snig* is assumed to represent a condition opposed in some way to *green*. The student would probably guess, without difficulty, that *snig* was an antonym of green in this sense and suggests *brown, withered, fallen,* or *dead,* etc.

The final step in the initial presentation of inference in English is to give the pupil longer contexts, in which he is required to check and compare his early guesses with repetitions of the same forms in later context. In this way, he learns to follow discussions, make intelligent guesses as he goes along, and then to amend automatically what he has guessed as more context is known.

Now the pupil is ready to proceed to target language texts. He now has a general idea of what his inferential process is in English and is ready to apply it to Spanish problems. The initial English presentation may have taken one or two class hours. The expansion into Spanish will require much more time, perhaps one or two class hours for each of the subdivisions of the initial English lesson we mentioned above. On the time distribution diagram for the advanced class, presented in Chapter 11, inference of meaning activities belong to the extensive reading portion of the block of time recommended for reading. Thus, if inference exercises are to be done regularly during an entire academic year, one class hour in ten is a comfortable minimum. If they are to be limited to the final semester, they should occupy one class hour in five. A reader designed for fourth-year use (or a second-year college reader) should be used as a corpus for the exercises. This assumes a

---

[5] L. Seibert, and L. G. Crocker, *Skills and Techniques of Reading French* (Baltimore: Johns Hopkins Press, n.d.). Refer to Stone and Paniagua, *Cuentos de Villarrica* (Boston: Blaisdell) which gives many drills to develop this technique of inference from context.

basic vocabulary of approximately 3,000 words. Investigators have shown that a basic vocabulary of only 2,000 words appears to be sufficient for successful exercises in inferring meaning. The teacher can then extract sections of three to four pages, underlining terms which he considers to be apt targets. The pupils, who should not be fore-warned or allowed to prepare themselves in any way, are then required to give an equivalent or descriptive definition of each of the terms. Following this, in class discussion, a justification for each choice should be given, in order to point up the process of inference that has taken place. It is unwise to select contexts from literary materials and the like, since students slow themselves down by trying to remember clues from foregoing chapters, the plot, characterization, etc.

In cases where no guess approximates the meaning of a form, the teacher should supply the correct definition. There should be no translation into English. The exercise is meant to develop the pupil's ability to infer in the target language. Where English is introduced in this activity, it tends to produce an effect counter to the purpose. Some teachers have attempted to use editions of daily newspapers in Spanish for these exercises but have found that contexts in journalistic style are unusually difficult, except for the most promising students.

► EXERCISES

1. Why must the powers of inference be developed in pupils, even when they have access to dictionaries and reference grammars?
2. How does the inference of meaning, as we have suggested here, parallel features of "natural" language learning, i.e., the way in which one learns one's native language?
3. Why do we suggest that an introduction to the inference of structural meaning (meaning conveyed by the position, inflection, and relationship of words) should precede stylistic meaning (meaning conveyed by the "sense" of the utterance)?
4. How important is the precise dictionary definition of passive vocabulary items in the learning of a second language?
5. Discuss the negative values implicit in the students' use of bilingual dictionaries.
6. Select an appropriate reading passage and develop a lesson of the type described in this chapter.

REFERENCE BOOKS AND ARTICLES

CARROLL, JOHN. "Words, Meaning, and Concepts" (*Harvard Educational Review* XXXIV, 1964), 178–202.

A B C D E F G H I J   5 4 3 2 1 7 0 6 9

PHOTOGRAPHY
On The Go
ROBT. L. WHITBY   WA 6-3049